The Military Takeover of America

by
Jay Cuze

Part I: Looking Forward

2016

Now, almost two years after the military takeover, I am amazed that I am still alive. Would disappointed be more accurate? Somehow, I'd imagined I'd be among the first to be taken away or simply shot outside the door of my home. I'd been among the first if not the first to prophesize a military take over. Spring of 2007 was the date I first posted the prediction on my blog. You may check it out—if my blog is still there on the net at http://abetterworld.blogspot.com. I haven't made any postings since 2014; it didn't seem prudent. But every chance I got, from the spring of 2007 on until the takeover itself, I would repeat my prediction on the bulletin boards I subscribed to.

Prior to 2014, I'd submitted frequent rants to the newspapers calling for more taxes on the wealthy to pay for our crumbling infrastructure. Yet, since the takeover I've never seen a sign of the gray-green fatigues, though tens of thousands have been disappeared, imprisoned, sent to camps. Some have been tortured then done away with. Some have been tortured, but allowed to live useless to the causes they had once represented, useless even to themselves. This is how we know. And me? I've been contacted only once and by a neighborhood patrol. The sad truth of the matter is that I am no more important after the takeover than I'd been before.

I'd imagined (assumed?) that one of my neighbors would show up at my door one day with a gun. I'd been the Democratic worker for my precinct after all, precinct Captain though I'd never been able to recruit a Lieutenant. I'd been outspoken politically, indifferent to talk of football, known at least locally, I'd thought for my progressive views. Apparently, my neighbors had thought differently. In their eyes, I was merely a harmless old coot, generous with the artichokes and tomatoes from his garden. Regardless, I kept a golf club close at hand. Golf club against gun, a guaranteed win with a pre-emptive strike on my part. But the men who showed up at my door one day were not neighbors, merely a band of opportunists and it was my neighbors who chased them away.

One of my neighbors did disappear, about a year ago. He was a Republican actually. Perhaps Libertarian would have been a better description had he been willing to accept the label. He was very difficult to agree with; any attempt at adopting his opinions would lead to an immediate rejection of the alliance. He was well to do, though he'd done a great deal to disguise it. Though he owned a half dozen rentals, his own home was a small one-story affair. I suspect he was not a particularly pleasant landlord and that one of his tenants had done away with them. His wife, an attractive blond woman, seemed content with his disappearance. Besides, everyone knew it would be useless to complain. The police in our town had a reputation for brutality before the takeover.

As far as my own acquaintances went, I'd had few to begin with. Most I'd known the past five or ten years only through email. None of our correspondence was interrupted, no more than usual as some acquired other interests. As far as I could tell from the communications I received, the disappearances had not affected them personally, had involved only persons they'd heard of but didn't actually know.

I'd known there were Muslims in Detroit or had been once, but I hadn't actually known any of them personally. And the use of their former Mosque as a barracks seemed a necessary cost-saving measure.

It was the spring of 2007, when I first realized that a military takeover in America was inevitable. Not that we weren't already halfway there. As early as the mid-fifties, Eisenhower had prophesied that the military-industrial complex would swallow our economy. Reading Chalmers Johnson a half-century later, I was to learn that the U.S. Air force had set up golf courses (with an adjoining air base as cover) in more than 90 countries. That the U.S. Army was Coca-Cola's biggest customer; Procter and Gamble's biggest customer, also.

The media also was the military's beneficiary. Other branches of government might have to be allotted pro bono public service announcements. The military paid for their commercials. The Marines even sponsored NBA games.

Our Defense Department purchased and used more

gasoline than any other customer and was the principal source of revenue for the Saudis. Billions each day were spent in Iraq and Afghanistan and all our troop movements required huge amounts of high-grade gasoline. No wonder our recent invasion of Canada was accomplished largely on foot and bicycle. Lacking funds in our even more depressed economy, our troops have learned to live off the land.

I chose 2014 as the probably date for the putsch, figuring that a Democrat would be elected President in 2008, but that the economy would have slid so far downhill by then that he would be unable to correct our nation's inevitable downward course. Nonetheless, despite my prediction, I thought at election time that maybe Obama could do something, could accomplish the seemingly impossible. He was young, not too set in his ways and with the nation behind him might be willing to risk the belt-tightening steps that would be necessary if we were to stay on course.

I was wrong, dead wrong about him, but so were millions of other voters. We did not get out of Iran as scheduled; instead, we invaded Afghanistan for the second time, a move which spelled disaster for our economy as it had for the lives and the livelihoods of Afghanistan's dozen and a half other invaders throughout history beginning with Tamerlane. (Genghis Khan was smart; he went around the country and captured everything else). Obama had promised we would leave Cuba, a country whose land we'd occupied as far back as the Spanish-American war—but no, we did not do that either. Had he been threatened? Or blackmailed? The first explanation seemed most reasonable; the military had thousands of trained assassins on call. To say nothing of the six years the Bush administration trained torturers at Guantanamo.

The true explanation of our successive invasions of Afghanistan and Iraq has remained elusive, though dozens of proposals abound. No weapons of mass destruction were found on invading Iraq, nor had anyone who read the newspapers (and remembered what was written there) expected to find them. Alas while I knew that the so-called justifications for our invasion of Iraq were lies, had known almost the moment they left Bush's lips, 35% of Americans still swore by their tattered legitimacy. As Robert Baer, a former CIA agent, reported in his book, *See No Evil,* Saddam had sold off all the weapons the first President Bush had given him within weeks of their receipt. As for the official pretext for invading Afghanistan to capture Osama bin Laden; somehow, despite the elderly bin Laden's being a late stage diabetic suffering from kidney failure so that he was in constant need of dialysis, we never did succeed in finding him.

The "alternative" explanations were equally suspect: We'd invaded Iraq so that Bush Jr. could rebuild Bush Sr.'s legacy and not incidentally, get his approval ratings back up. The Taliban having destroyed so many of the poppy fields, our invasion of Afghanistan was to get the heroin back on the streets. This latter rationale must also be given some credence for indeed the heroin did return to our streets in quantity and when the Taliban needed money to finance their cause, they'd no choice but to encourage poppy cultivation.

The fact remains that whatever these wars' true rationale, their end result was to further expand the military's power and to further shift our nation's wealth from the hands of the many to the hands of the few. In the pages that follow, I shall try to trace the inevitability of the takeover and to trace its progress to date. I'll contrast the takeover with the military takeovers in the South American countries of Brazil, Chile, and Uruguay. Though the U.S. military was implicated in all three, and all were followed by mass arrests and disappearances, all three countries eventually returned to civilian rule.

Our discussion will include events that took place in the 1970s and earlier, but our main focus will be on the actions and policies of the neoconservatives during the preceding decade.

Should my samdizat treatise survive, the first questions future generations will ask of it are the first I respond to in the following chapters: What led to the military takeover? Why did a people inured to centuries of self-rule yield so readily to autocrats? Was there no resistance? And, if there was, what was its nature?

Causes

If asked to name the reasons why a country, that throughout its entire history had provided a beacon of religious and political freedom for the balance of the world, should abruptly yield to a military dictatorship, a single phrase leaps to mind:

It's the economy stupid.

We've all heard the story of the 26-year-old who back in 2010 had to suspend her photography and sculpture career because her parents could no longer support her. "My artistic career is put on the side because I have to make a living."

But focusing on a single cause for our tragedy would be misleading. True, the sharp decline into bankruptcy that accompanied the Bush administration's neoconservative policies was among the chief reasons democracy failed in America, accompanied as it was by a lack of jobs, an abrupt decline in personal income, and the feeling that we were somehow second rate as individuals and as a nation.

Still, this was not the first depression our country had experienced. Nor was it the first in which the very wealthy behaved in flagrant disregard of the needs of the middle class. But it was the first in which those most responsible for bringing about the system's failure were able to run an extensive and successful program of disinformation.

We were told by the right wing to worry about welfare fraud, though the fraud perpetrated in military contracts in Iraq and in rebuilding after Hurricane Katrina was a thousand times greater.

Some of us had gone without work for more than a year, had lost our homes, our health insurance, yet our taxpayer money was used not to create jobs, but to bail out a dozen failed banks whose officers subsequently received bonuses of fifty million dollars or more apiece! Fifty million! Fifty dollars would have meant another month of cable for a family or a meal at a good restaurant to raise the flagging spirits of a man and his wife. Five hundred would have covered my monthly mortgage, while five thousand per month was required for the mortgages of the many who'd been tempted in the previous five years to buy beyond their means. Fifty million could have made the payments on 10,000 mortgages, kept 10,000 families in their homes!

Congress has always been corrupt, as witness Mark Twain's acerbic comments on the 19th Century version of that august body. But never before had its members, suppositories all jammed firmly up the assholes of the multinational corporations, been quite so shameless, so indifferent to the needs or the opinions of their constituents.

Congressmen's votes could be and traditionally were purchased by big-money interests. From the founding of the American Republic to the middle of the 20th century, these were our own American-born interests, or own multimillionaires. But beginning in the 1950's, as an adjunct to Marshall Aid, Congress began to get on the payroll of foreign nations. Today, our elected representatives are the beneficiaries of corporations, governments, and individuals who bear little or no loyalty to the U.S.A. electorate.

Today, foreign interests are permitted to own and operate our domestic media—newspapers, TV stations, and radio. And as we will see later in this chapter, China has taken full advantage of this loophole.

From 2008 through 2010, layoffs by and closures of our domestic corporations continued for more than two years until 15% of the population was unemployed (25% if we exclude the military from these calculations), yet the number of foreign workers admitted legally was permitted to double during the Bush years. From the few point of their multinational corporate employers, these foreign workers were a bonus. Skilled workers in the main, they were willing to labor for half the wages our native-born engineers, programmers, professors and other professionals had grown accustomed to.

Work was to be had, the right-wing media critics declared, if only one looked hard enough. Work at McDonalds or some other fast-food restaurant? Not if one couldn't speak the language, couldn't relate to one's illegal coworkers. For at the behest of the corporations, illegals poured across our porous borders, and enforcement of the laws against their employment were rare indeed.

Given the engagement of Abraham Lincoln's administration in a war he did not want, he'd felt he had no choice but to institute a tax on incomes. This tax would be graduated according to the taxpayer's income, for, as Lincoln put it, those who gained the most from this country and its wars ought pay the most for its support. A century and a half later, in a parody of basic economics, Bush Lite launched a series of wars our nation did not need and proposed to pay for them by reducing the taxes on the rich. The not unexpected result was a deeper deficit and economic ruin for our nation.

Why did we not protest? The ruling Romans used circuses to divert their populace. Our ruling classes offer Jerry Springer, Fox News, and Reality TV.

Terry Gilliam's film *Brazil* proved prophetic as we found ourselves threatened daily with terrorist attacks. Bush's newly appointed Homeland Security Tsar sounded a series of red, yellow, and orange alerts. Civil liberty was sacrificed to survival.

Let's take another closer look at the differences and similarities between then and the now of 2011.

1. **Establishment of a Military-Industrial Complex**. During World War II, the manufacturers of weapons and military equipment had seen immense profits. They were never to forgo such profits again. Our isolationist right suddenly developed a strong interest in foreign affairs. Our troops went to Korea, then to Vietnam, then to

Columbia and Iraq. As the 20th century ended and peace was finally in our grasp, we enlarged our army and sent our troops—with inferior and often inappropriate arms and equipment, into the Middle East. Under Bush, it was decreed that we would purchase weapons without testing them.

2. **Rise of the Right Wing**. Curiously our entry into the war in 1941 was never assured. Powerful right wing forces (encouraged and often subsidized by Germany) were at work to forestall our entry. The novel, *Fatherland,* depicts a mythical future in which Joseph Kennedy became President in 1940 and kept America neutral. The attacks on Roosevelt at that time are echoed in their ferocity by the attacks on Obama today (encouraged and often subsidized by China). The big distinction was

3. **Centralized Media**. In the olden days, our media was decentralized. The media was partisan then as now but as it was in the hands of hundreds of individuals with half a dozen newspapers and a dozen independently owned TV and radio stations in each major market, hundreds of points of view were expressed. Today, our media is national rather than regional in scope. As it costs far more to insert a story in a national medium than in a local paper and few but the very rich can afford it. Moreover, foreign interests can and do purchase time on our airwaves. One country, China, owns a TV/radio/and newspaper network Fox, outright.

4. **The Dumbing Down of Education**. In the 19th and early 20th century, even elementary school students were fully aware of the crises that had given rise to our nation. Our ancestors, they learned, had come to America from Europe seeking religious freedom. For in England and throughout Western Europe in the 17th and 18th Centuries, the major religions—Anglicans, Catholics, Lutherans, Puritans and Presbyterians had in common a fervent desire to see the members of all other religions tortured, imprisoned and put to death. America's founding fathers resolved that hatred would be put aside, religious freedom and freedom of speech guaranteed. To the rest of the world we became a beacon of intellectual and religious liberty. Today, our students may remain aware that we are or once were such a beacon, but are no longer told why. (Check the state of your own knowledge via *Lies My Teacher Told Me* by James Lowen.)

5. **Guns.** One non-factor in the acceptance of the takeover, though one often favored by psychologists, is the prevalence of guns in civilian hands. In 2004 alone, 29,569 Americans died by gunfire: 16,750 in firearm suicides, 11,935 in firearm homicides, 649 in unintentional shootings, and 235 in firearm deaths of unknown intent, according to the National Center for Health Statistics. More than twice this number are treated in emergency rooms each year for nonfatal firearm injuries.

Yet the rate of firearms mortality peeked in the 1970's and has actually declined by one-third since that time. The percentage of American households that report having any guns in the home dropped nearly 20 percentage points from a high of 54 percent in 1977 to 34.5 percent in 2006.

A psychological factor that may well have desensitized us to violence is our long exposure to mayhem and gun play, real as well as fictional, via the television and other news media. No public outcry arose against our use of torture against enemy combatants during the unending war in Iraq and it was but a small further step toward our acceptance of the use of torture today against those the government labels as "the enemies amongst us." (Our torturers are highly skilled. Latin America has looked to us for instruction since the 1970's. And during the Bush administration we raised a bumper crop of our own in Guantanamo Bay.)

6. **China and our policy of unilateral free trade**. Perhaps the act most destructive to US interests that Nixon committed during his Presidency was to open the door to China. That grandiose half-wit was completely outsmarted for the door proved to open in one direction only. China-made goods poured into the U.S. at bargain prices, putting many of our companies out of business and a multitude of our workers out of jobs. The U.S. gained nothing in return; neither our advice nor our goods and services were wanted. How could China make goods so cheaply? By using convicts and members of their army, practices our own country had abandoned until this past year.

Taking the role the CIA played in South America's military takeovers of the 1970's were both China's Communist-controlled civilian spy agency MSS, the Ministry of State Security, and its military counterpart, the Second Department of the People's Liberation Army, or 2PLA.

These two as well as other branches of China's government also exercised a more direct role. They bribed Congressmen and presidential advisers. A costly stimulus package of $300 per person during the Bush administration led to dramatic increases in the sale of Chinese made goods, while sales of heavy equipment made in the USA remained flattened or stalled completely. They invested heavily in U.S. securities and are among the United States major creditors. The costly bank bailouts of 2008 and 2009 were largely the result of pressure from the Chinese.

In 1999, as a result of Rupert Murdoch's marriage to Chinese-born Deng Wendi, Fox News and other Murdoch-dominated media in the U.S. and abroad took an even more dramatic turn to the right. The objective from China's point of view was to destabilize the American government. For as long as America remained a democracy, there would always be pressure on the Chinese government to relax its own dictatorial policies. Not incidentally, the role of the MSS is also to bolster Beijing's Communist Party rule by repressing religious and political dissent. Thus the steady flow of disinformation emanating from the Murdoch Empire.

Finally, the virtual abandonment of inspections of cargo from abroad under the Bush administration permitted the importation of dangerous and defective goods from China. The long terms effects on the health and economy of our people, as in the case of toxic wallboard, are just beginning to be felt.

7. **The Magic Pill**. The efforts of French bacteriologists in the 1920's led to the near eradication of tuberculosis in Japan, Eastern Europe, and France, a literal gift to the poor. Dr Albert Sabin, a Jewish Polish-American, aided by the Russian government, developed the oral vaccine that has led to the near eradication of polio. (Curiously, through the extensive pubic-relations efforts of the March of Dimes purchased with the tax-free donations they'd received from Americans, we were led to believe that the research of Jonas Salk the March of Dimes had sponsored led to the cure, when in fact the Salk vaccine gave polio and leukemia to thousands. This would not be the last time in America that public relations efforts would successfully place a positive spin on disaster, as the administrations of Nixon, Reagan, and Bush soon revealed.) But it was the efforts of chemists at Syntex and Searle that were to totally revolutionize the American way of life and set the stage for our present predicament.

The pill put women in charge of their lives. Smaller families were the immediate result. No longer was a woman be obliged to bear children until the male parent had a male heir.

Smaller families meant that post-pill children had greater attention lavished upon them and grew up with a sense of privilege and entitlement. In former times, the oldest child would have been forced to move out of the family home to make room for his younger still-growing siblings. Now he or she was permitted to stay still living off the family dole. Or, if he or she left, she would be permitted to return after first trying out life in the cruel world. These post-pill children became our boomerang generation. All had in common the expectation that their government, taking the place of their parents, would continue to offer extensive benefits at no cost to them. Uncivil discourse, the threat as well as the actuality of violence our society experienced throughout 2010 were merely a symptom, not a cause. Our grownup children wanted representation without taxation and were encouraged in this belief by the very rich, who, not incidentally, owned all the major media.

Curiously, a half-century earlier, it was the far right wing in the form of the John Burch Society that had plastered billboards all over the Southern United States, with a portrait of Uncle Sam and a legend reading, "He's not your father, he's your uncle." Of course, the ultra-rich, responding to a proposal from a till-then lethargic Democratic administration to raise their taxes beginning in 2011, might well have been responsible for the timing of the takeover.

2014: The Takeover

In contrast to the CIA-inspired military coups that had taken place in Latin America in the 1970's (concerning which I will write more in a later chapter), the military take-over of our vast nation appeared to be spontaneous (though I've no doubt it had been on the military's planning boards if only as a War College or a Northern Command exercise for more than half a century) and was widely dispersed both in space and time.

The proximate cause was a series of protests in State capitals and outside the centers of government in the larger cities. Initially, these protests were carried out either by government workers protesting cuts in pay (essential if state and local budgets were to be balanced without an increase in taxes) or ratepayers demanding cuts in taxes. If such protests extended into a second or third day, counter protestors were sure to put in an appearance. In times past, particularly in the 1910's, 1930's, and late 1960's, armed police would have quickly brought an end to the protests. In 2014, the police practiced great restraint, standing on the sidelines while civil discourse turned to violence.

The revolution was televised. The day following each media revelation, other, many other irate citizens would join protestors and counter-protestors with different and distinct axes to grind. Say, one's father had been ill-treated in a nursing home. You could join the picket lines to demand both closer regulation and lower taxes, siding with whichever group of protestors seemed most receptive to your conflicting needs.

When guns and axe handles appeared in civilian hands as they inevitably did, martial law would be declared. In some areas, an active police presence was sufficient to bring a stop to the demonstrations and counter demonstrations. In others, the Governor of the State would need to call upon the National Guard or the Northern Command to intervene.

New York City simply imploded. It held too many cultures, too many ethnicities, had too wide a gap between its rich and its poor. Did the riots begin when a frustrated commuter threw a cup of hot coffee at a slow-moving barista? Or punched a man who had jumped the line? You could run but you could not hide. The police, though held back at first, were brought out en masse when the Governor of the New York State declared martial law. Federal involvement was immediate.

In the Southern States, it was black against white, with the unemployed (white or black) strongly resenting the employed of the opposite color whom they came in contact with whenever they were forced to buy a stamp, renew a driver's license, or pay a traffic ticket. The South, with its strong tradition of military service for whites and military employment for blacks, greeted the Army as a conquered people might greet its liberators. The immediate deaths were few.

In the Mountain States, farmers and freeholders set

about burning down the second homes of the idle rich, whom they felt had invaded their territory. When an environmentalist stood in front of a tractor, he was run over. When ten environmentalists replaced their deceased comrade, the freeholders' guns came out. The normally reclusive former Vice-President Dick Cheney appeared at a Montana community college to declare his support for the violence, only to be shot dead by a long-distance rifle. The shooter was never identified; was he a communist as alleged or merely another irate farmer. The crowd set about killing everyone in sight, students as well as professors, including many of their own children. The Air Force appeared, leveled the campus, and restored order, at least momentarily, to the entire Mountain Region.

Occasional clashes between right wing militias and government troops did break out in Wyoming and Montana in succeeding months and were usually resolved by the troops yielding the disputed area to the militia. But such retreats on the part of the regional government were deceptive. When attempts were made to enlarge a militia's boundaries or to further assert the militia's independence, an entire division of regular troops would be brought in and ruthlessly crush the revolt.

In some instances, particularly in the mid-West, martial law was declared by the local authorities well before the arrival of any troops. Anti-war protestors and avowed socialists were rounded up and imprisoned, again strictly on the local authorities own initiative. Deaths were limited strictly to those who resisted. In other sections of the country, particularly in the Southwest and Mountain States, what best might be described as class warfare broke out; the homes of the upper middle class were targeted along with those of perceived intellectuals. The truly wealthy were well protected with troops and local police assigned to protect their homes, though many employed armed guards as well.

In Los Angeles and San Francisco, violence erupted on the borders between communities, black and Hispanic, black and Asian. As with the original Watts riots, the authorities allowed these conflicts to resolve themselves, though blacks that ventured into white enclaves were apprehended quickly. At least initially, no intervention by federal authorities could be justified.

The ultimate takeover of the "West" or, as popular expression had it, "Left" Coast entailed a quite different approach. First, radio and television warned of potential attacks by the Chinese. Soon, our Pacific Fleet appeared at ports up and down the coast, from San Diego to Seattle, much to the gratitude of the inhabitants. Our Navy bombers, turned back from butterflies to once again ride shotgun in the sky, were greeted with equal enthusiasm. Martial law was declared. Dissidents were rounded up, and the Navy assumed control. Then and only then, with the entire nation under military rule, did the real slaughter begin.

2015: Under Military Rule

"Because throwing bodies in the San Gabriel River is creating problems for coastal residents, such as the appearance of mutilated cadavers on the beaches, crematorium ovens from the state hospitals shall be used for the incineration of subversives who die in captivity."

> Directive 117, West Coast Military Authority

The military takeover was perhaps not quite so straightforward as I've described. Voices of dissent were raised but were as quickly herded by the Army into the stadiums. Some dissenters were slaughtered by right wing extremists in the name of freedom. Under cover of the initial curfews, the satisfaction of personal grudges was also common. While most demonstrations could be resolved with a shot or two, in areas where redevelopment had been postponed in times past on grounds of environmental, historical, or social interest, tanks would be brought in, and buildings where snipers might be lurking razed to the ground.

Once the violence subsided, the military government made a careful series of graduated changes. First, the wages paid government workers as well as the minimum wage were brought in line with military pay, never mind that those in the armed services also received free board and lodging as well as free medical care. The advantages of belonging to a union were lost immediately; union organizers who protested were termed "unamerican" even by their fellow workers; persistent protestors were taken away, imprisoned, tortured and/or killed.

The provisions of 2010's Health Reform bill that benefited the public were reversed; those that benefited the insurance companies were retained. Surprisingly, veteran's benefits were not increased; to receive government largess one had to be on active duty. Several of the top-performing VA hospitals were reclassified as Military Hospitals and, again, were open to active military only. "The military," as one reckless civilian remarked, "has its own brand of socialism."

Social Security was privatized. The monthly payment seniors made for Medicare, privatized since its inception in 1965, were increased and the benefits reduced. Add-on insurance coverage (that excluded pre-existing conditions) was available for a price. "Man is free to buy or not to buy," declared one economic theorist, a disciple of the late Milton Friedman.

Rent controls in the major cities were abolished. Young professionals, still paying off college loans, were obliged to double up a second or even a third time. Or, as some soon did, to sign long term contracts with the military. Dance studios were abandoned for lack of customers, while bars that offered free dance lessons were packed nightly. Off, off-Broadway productions starved for lack of actors.

The major corporations and their major stockholders, the manufacturers of weapons, of troop carriers, of Coca-Cola, Marlboroughs, toothpaste and toilet paper, for whom the Army had always been their best customer, remained closely allied with the new regime, much as the same manufacturers (though absent specific brands like Coke and Marlborough) had remained closely allied with the forces of the Third Reich. Politicians, though no longer needing to serve, continued to receive their Congressional salaries for some time, along with the payments from the Army and the major corporations that always been their primary source of revenue.

No other nation interfered with the takeover or, it seemed, did they care to. For Latin America and Western Europe, the change meant that the pushy Americans would finally get their comeuppance. Our arrogant interference in the internal affairs of other countries over the preceding half century had resulted in a deep-seeded hatred of all Americans. Later, when our military government cut off all non-military travel abroad, and our tourist dollars were no longer available, these nations would have second thoughts.

As for the dictatorial regimes, China, North Korea, and the Mid-East sheikdoms welcomed the change as it meant the United States would no longer be forcing democracy upon them. Chinese authorities rubbed their hands in glee. Had not Mao said to Nixon, "I like a man on the right?" Their investment in spreading disinformation via American media had paid off big time.

Geopolitics

Freed from political constraints, the Army was able to get all the troops it needed for domestic occupation by withdrawing them from Afghanistan, Iraq, and Saudi Arabia. When the Pacific Fleet pulled back to occupy and defend our West Coast, China responded with a successful invasion of its long-sought island of Taiwan. North Korea again sought to invade South Korea, albeit less successfully. After a delay of several months in which the Koreans took hundreds of thousands of casualties on both sides, China entered from the north to announce that both Koreas could now consider themselves part of a Greater Chinese Co-Prosperity sphere. As the Koreans, South as well as North, were now desperate for food as well as peace, they were quickly absorbed. The few Koreans (mainly from the south) that were still disaffected found few countries willing to accept them despite the funds they brought with them.

Iran procrastinated but eventually decided that it too would risk an invasion given that the United States Armed Forces otherwise occupied. They sent several divisions across the border into southern Iraq. As that part of Iraq is majority Shiite as is Iran, resistance to the invading Shiite troops was minimal. But rather than advancing farther north toward Baghdad as might well have been expected, Iran's armies then crossed into the Sunni stronghold of Saudi Arabia. Their objective was to bring an end to the centuries-old conflict between the two branches of Islam. Alas, they completely misread the U.S.'s intentions. A USAF squadron based in Turkmenistan joined by Naval aircraft from carriers in the Arabian Sea proceeded to bomb Iran's military installations, destroying all nuclear power stations in Southern and Western Iran, while Russian bombers poured in from the North to complete the process

The declaration of peace was accompanied by an agreement on Iran's part to permit the exploration of its oil fields by American and Russian firms. A revolt against Iran's totalitarian theocracy by its more moderate inhabitants is ongoing and a much weakened, nuclear-weapon-free Iran is expected to rejoin the company of nations.

2016: Under Military Rule

Innumerable large-scale projects were launched this year and last: high-speed rail lines, desalinization plants, flood channels and levees along the Mississippi–though few have actually gone to completion. "Voluntary" pay cuts have been imposed on educators. In some areas, all government appointments including school teachers and army officers go to the highest bidders.

Though lip service is given by the military government to the effect theirs is a market-based economic system, one in which the private sector is the engine of growth, in fact, it represents a continuation of the failed economic policies of the Bush neo-conservative administration, the very same policies that led to the collapse of the American economy four years ago as well as that of the Chilean economy, thirty years earlier. No new taxes have been imposed on the well to do, while monies collected from the middle class in the form of taxes and "voluntary" contributions invariably end in the hands of a few, very few government supporters. Privatizing social security is but one example.

Consolidation in business is everywhere; it was as if even the very rich are playing a form of winner take all. Before the takeover, California had three major grocery chains and a handful of independents; a short time later the three were reduced to two and these soon made inroads on the independents by setting up secondary chains that specialized in organic and health foods.

Apart from setting limits on wages and reducing taxes on corporations and capital gains, the government has abstained from interference in the economy. Admittedly for some retail outlets and restaurants providing discounts for servicemen in uniform (or those claiming to be servicemen) has become one of the costs of doing business. Prices on all goods, particularly day-to-day necessities–meat, flour, cooking oil, have risen. Fortunately, goods made in China are still available and even more affordable now that their inspection has been discontinued again. (Note added in proof: with the recent revaluation of Chinese currency, the cost of foreign-made goods has doubled in some instances.)

Our poor have gotten steadily poorer, surviving in some instances only by selling body parts, late-term fetuses, newborns, and one another. Disease is rampant among them as public health programs have been abandoned. The CDC (Centers for Disease Control and Prevention) in Atlanta was reclassified as military and its benefits limited to the military. State Public Health Agencies that relied on the CDC might have complained had their funding not dried up. Vaccinations against flu and childhood diseases are available free to members of the military and their families and must be purchased otherwise if available.

Though the science of medicine has continued to make broad advances, medical care is more and more limited to the well to do. The gap between rich and poor has become, as it was two centuries before, a gap is between the well and the sick, the living and the dead. A new class of private contractors (all paid with government funds) has arisen dedicated to corpse removal.

From time to time, attempts have been made by do-gooders to form cooperatives, which would serve its members by purchasing groceries and other necessary items in bulk. Such cooperatives are legal in theory, but a great deal of paperwork was require and approval might be delayed indefinitely.

To be fair, some efforts have been made lately to care for the poor. Reclaimed water in bulk can be purchased from dispensers outside almost every grocery store. Toxic waste dumps taken over by the government have been covered over and shanty towns permitted to spring up on their surface while a decision is made regarding the dumps' final disposition. In urban areas, once houses and apartment blocks have been condemned, the poor are permitted to squat inside them, pending rebuilding. Strangely, in instances where homes had been abandoned, perhaps because all their former occupants were dead, disappeared, in jail, or had fled the country, rather than given to the dispossessed, they have been taken over by eminent domain, then resold to the highest bidder.

Street beggars have begun to appear in large numbers in city centers and suburban shopping malls, the majority of them children. As the Orange County Register reports, "the money is quickly taken away from them by their parents. The authorities should put an immediate halt to this practice."

Some localities have contracted with private firms to round up and remove offenders. An unmarked panel truck will pull up near a corner where beggars have gathered, a few men armed with batons and clubs will herd them into the back of the van and then they are driven away. With luck, they will be taken to the edge of the district where the contractor is employed and released for a competing firm to handle.

When Libertarians and college-educated Young Americans for Freedom (the youth wing of the Republican party) professed to speak out on behalf of the people, they were shot on the spot. Neighborhood cleansing focused on the over-educated as well. Though no one ever broke into a doctor's office, many doctors have been shot only a few blocks from their homes. The army had no choice but to step in and stem the flood of seemingly random killings (though in every case it was clearly us against them, with each individual having his or her own definition of who "us" and "them" were.)

In contrast to the military takeover in Chile, when mass arrests and disappearances had taken place immediately, the military in America bided its time. In 2015, they began slowly and methodically to work from lists rounding up individuals to question or to intern. Occasionally, they might seize suspects from the wrong address, but such collateral damage was minor.

Right-wing extremists, whether acting alone or in groups, were less discriminating. Mexicans soon learned not to wait by the roadside hoping for jobs. Muslims, Orthodox Jews, and Sikhs made easy targets because of their headgear. The owners and occupants of automobiles bearing peace symbols and pleas for gun control were singled out for destruction. Asians and other minorities in small communities and on the borders between urban villages were pursued and beaten. Sensibly, Samoans were left alone.

Still, the only solution to the wide-spread unemployment (which the military take-over has done nothing to resolve) is the by-now tried and true method of singling out a segment of the population for destruction, confiscating their wealth, and redistributing it among the faithful. As always, the obvious choices are Muslims and Jews, though some favor killing or imprisoning Mexicans or Asians. Fox News vehemently opposed killing Chinese and business leaders made their need to retain cheap immigrant labor widely known. So it was back to Muslims and Jews with bribes readily accepted from both sides. Truthfully, bribes were also accepted from Asian communities. As African-Americans were present in the army in disproportionate numbers, they were left alone.

Jews or Muslims? The majority of senior army officers were both anti-Semitic by upbringing and pro-Israel as a result of the joint exercises they'd engaged in with the Israeli military and the mutual respect this had developed. . The idea of a *soft* return was floated by the Israeli government: any Jew that could be identified as such along with anyone who was willing to be identified as a Jew would be allowed to migrate to Israel, sans their possessions. The Israeli's replied that the idea was a fine one, in theory, but that they would need to expand into the Arab-occupied lands in order to house all the newcomers. They'd need the missing possessions also if they were to maintain any kind of standard of living for their existing population..

Abandoning this idea, the military immediately carried out a preemptive strike on the Arab enclaves in and around Detroit, transporting those who survived to a camp in eastern Colorado. As expected, the Saudis and Syrians protested, the Iranians too, threatening to cut off all shipments of oil. A compromise was reached: any Arab-American or Iranian who so requested would be allowed to return to his homeland at his government's expense and in return the oil would continue to flow. The Detroit Arabs, forgotten, joined the disappeared.

No counter revolution would materialize. Nor would any other nation interfere. It appears our entire population of child-like adults intent on instant gratification is just as satisfied they've finally been set non-negotiable boundaries. Dissatisfied are those who want the government to add to or eliminate existing environmental or social regulations. It seems the military government had no intention of involving itself in aspects of governance that it still views as "civilian concerns."

They also dithered with regard to the status of homosexuals despite pressure from the Christian right. Policies varied from region to region depending on the region's commanding officer. The only individuals to suffer were the residents of Boystown in Chicago when Major General Rumple decided on his own to have them evacuated.

Enforcement of the narcotic laws has also varied from region to region. The West Coast authorities reasoned, correctly, that while domestic marijuana contributed to the economy, imported cocaine did not. Stepped up patrols on land and sea, dynamiting of border tunnels, and close inspection of all landed cargo eliminated the imports. Marijuana was taxed; growers and retailers were licensed. Tax evaders and those guilty of driving or reporting for duty under the influence were jailed.

Though our borders are now sealed–at least in an outward bound direction–and visas nearly impossible to get, it is still possible to sneak across the border into Mexico, despite all the additional fencing and alarms. From Mexico, it is easy as always to get to Cuba, and from Cuba to Canada, and from Canada anywhere one might want to go. Escape of sorts is possible for the young and attractive, men as well as women. The more reliable employment agencies will see that the families of these individuals always receive payment.

I believe that pockets of dissidents must exist both here and abroad. Though many of the rebellious on both the right and the left had been slaughtered outright (as well as some few apolitical individuals who refused to make voluntary contributions), some may have escaped to hide, then, gradually, coalesce with their fellow rebels again. I do know, for I've heard from some of them, that escape is possible. It is this last that made me suspicious of our regime's ultimate intentions. Quislings exist in every country. A few in Canada have been cooperating with the American authorities for years. What if the regime decided to expand our borders? What then?

We've had no news of assassinations abroad, not that we could rely on our own newspapers to report them. So whatever our military's future plans might be, at the moment they've no intention of parroting the Pinochet regime's campaign of mass murder. Is this a healthy sign? My own view is that while our military, unlike our CIA, does not waste its energy on individuals; at some time in the future, the dissidents they've identified here and abroad will serve as black ewes to lead the other sheep to slaughter. Only, when the size of a dissident group justifies the expenditure of men and materiel will our government strike.

Parallels

A sensible person lives in the here and now. At my advanced age, a concern for the future is probably misplaced. Still, one cannot help but feel apprehensive. What does the future hold? What further changes will take place? Will the civilian-led republic be restored, if not in our lifetime, in that of our children's?

Some say that the military takeover of 2011 was fifty years in the making, the natural outgrowth of Operation Condor. Before speculating on he future of our own country, we ought consider the events that took place preceding and following the military takeovers in other countries, events, which in Latin America, were directly affected by American intervention.

The communist governments of China, Cuba, Russia, and Vietnam all came to power via their armies. Yet in each instance, the subsequent government immediately transitioned to civilian one-party rule. One could argue that Chairman Mao and First-Secretary Castro were both once generals of victorious armies, but they served subsequently as civilian heads of state. The same is true of our own Generals and Presidents Washington, Grant, and Eisenhower.

The exception to the rule is Burma/Myanmar whose communist government has been under the control of a military junta since 1962.

In the Latin American countries of Argentina, Chile, and Uruguay, the events leading up to a military takeover were more or less the same, varying only in timing and duration. The gap between rich and poor was far greater in these countries than in the United States before the takeover, and had persisted far longer. Only Argentina had a relatively large middle class. The United States also had a large established middle class; still, during the years of the Bush administration it came to bear a disproportionate portion of the tax burden, while the rich got richer.

In Chile, almost a year to the day after President Allende's election, some five thousand of the wealthiest women, some in party dresses, some accompanied by their maids and servants, some bedecked in jewels staged "the March of the Empty Pots" banging loudly on pots and pans as they went while crying out that they were hungry. That is, the best-fed, best-clothed, fattest and wealthiest people in Chile, as did the best insured of the U.S. in 2009 and 2010, alleged non-existent grievances.

Prior to the takeover, Chile had one party on the right and two on the left, the Socialists and the Communists. The United States had two established parties in Congress. As the Health Care debate in the U.S. in 2009 and 2010 revealed, while one party, the Republicans, could clearly be labeled the party of the right, the Democrat party, nominally in control of congress, were right, left and every flavor in between. It held progressives who favored a public option, centrists who would go along with any suggestion of the President, and Congressman so much on the take from special interests that they might best be described as suppositories. The corporations soon resolved the standoff. The high rate of unemployment made those who still had jobs almost slavish in their embrace of corporate interests. While a Supreme Court ruling that granted corporations the rights of individuals to provide political contributions ensured that the media would forever be the corporations' captive.

In Uruguay prior to the military takeover, political representation was similar to that of the United States in 2009. The legislature was divided between two parties neither of which might have been said to represent the people of Uruguay and its bad government was getting steadily worse with the economic situation steadily deteriorating. About a fifth of the population relied on government salaries and government pensions. Tax evasion, false bookkeeping, corruption in the granting of contracts, and excessive expenditures by government officials and legislators was widespread. The takeover in both countries consisted more of a yielding of power by the civilian government to the military, an autogope or self-coup, rather than a military coup. Yet, contrary to the events in our own country, in which the takeover was largely met with enthusiasm, in Uruguay a general strike ensued, thousands marched in the streets of Montevideo, and thousands were massacred or taken prisoner.

Argentina had a lengthy history of military coup d'etats. In 1951, a successful coup d'état against Juan Perón's democratically elected government took place, leading to the proscription of Peronism by the Armed forces. Peronist Resistance began organizing itself soon after the coup, in workplaces and trade unions. Over time, as democratic rule was partially restored but when promises of legalizing the expression and political liberties for Peronism were not respected, guerrilla groups started to appear. By the early seventies, military and police officers were robbed of their guns, kidnapped or even killed in Peronist and leftist guerilla actions almost weekly

As the armed struggle increased, the right wing launched the so-called "Dirty War" including the large-scale application of torture and rape, the intent, they alleged being "to maintain social order and eradicate political subversives." (A declaration echoed in our own country at the beginning of the 21st Century by then Vice-President Cheney.) Extreme right-wing death squads used their hunt for far-left guerrillas as a pretext to exterminate any and all ideological opponents on the left and as a cover for common crimes. Assassinations and kidnappings by the Peronist Montoneros and the ERP contributed to the general climate of fear.

In 1975, in a move which ought to have forestalled a military takeover, the recently-elected President Isabel Martínez de Perón, a right-wing Peronist, who had replaced the previous President, a left-wing Peronist, signed a series of decrees empowering the military and the police to annihilate left-wing subversion. Regardless, in 1976, a coup d'état by a military junta overthrew

Peron.

The United States had a hand in all the Latin American takeovers. In 1971, at the direction of President Nixon, the United States provided the out-of-power right-wing opposition in Chile with money and technical assistance. Along with France and Britain, we continued to provide behind the scenes support to the dictatorship for 16 more years, despite our public hand wringing over the dictatorship's human rights violations.

Two days after the coup in Argentina in 1976 that overthrew the recently-elected President Isabel Martínez de Perón, the U.S. Assistant Secretary of State for Latin America, William D. Rogers, stated, "I think also we've got to expect a fair amount of repression, probably a good deal of blood, in Argentina before too long. I think they're going to have to come down very hard not only on the terrorists but on the dissidents of trade unions and their parties." Secretary of State Henry Kissinger stated that "Whatever chance they [the junta] have, they will need a little encouragement" and "because I do want to encourage them. I don't want to give the sense that they're harassed by the United States."

Do we need wonder why there is little prospect that either of these countries will assist us, though once again they are democracies?

A transition to civilian government took place in Argentina, Brazil, Chile, and Uruguay at just about the same point in time and for much the same reason: An economic crisis was precipitated by the rising cost of oil and the usurious practices of the International Monetary Fund.

In Argentina, serious economic problems, mounting charges of corruption, public discontent and, finally, the country's 1982 defeat by the United Kingdom in the Falklands War all combined to discredit the Argentine military regime. Under strong public pressure, the junta lifted bans on political parties and gradually restored basic political liberties. The country returned to constitutional rule in 1983 following elections.

In Uruguay, GDP fell some 20 percent between 1981 and 1983, and unemployment rose to 17 percent. The foreign debt burden, exacerbated by the quadrupling of oil prices in 1974, grew exponentially and stood at about US$3 billion by 1984.

The yielding of power to a constitutional government during the period was done reluctantly, with imprisonment of opposition leaders and their torture continuing almost up to the day of elections. (Indeed, many who had been taken prisoner at the start of military rule were still in jail.) In 1983 the Interunion Workers' Assembly (PIT) was permitted by the military government to hold a public demonstration on May 1. Students united under the Asociación Social y Cultural de Estudiantes de la Enseñanza Pública were allowed to march through the streets of Montevideo. In November all opposition parties including the left staged a massive political rally, demanding elections with full restoration of democratic norms and without political proscriptions.

The military procrastinated, but yielded power after succeeding in prohibiting some candidates from running in the initial elections and negotiating freedom from prosecution for its members.

In Chile, military rule, under a single dictator rather than a committee, persisted until 1990. This despite a collapse of domestic industrial production due to yet another of the dictatorship's failed economic policies in 1982 when the GNP plummeted by 14%, and unemployment reached 33%. A series of public protests beginning in May 1983 involving primarily the poor and the disenfranchised was quickly suppressed. Occasionally riot police would venture into the slums (the source of most of the protests) and fire indiscriminately at anyone within range. The disappearances and preliminary torture continued. Anti-government guerrillas conducted sporadic attacks against military and the police. And the police and army would hunt them down.

Negotiations with regard to the dictator's status after the restoration of partial democracy continued throughout the 1980's. Under pressure from the Catholic Church as well as the U.S., Pinochot's staunch supporter till they heard he was planning to renege on the amounts Chile owed to the IMF, Pinochot offered his countrymen the "opportunity "to vote in a yes-or-no referendum for a single candidate for president chosen by the dictator. No one doubted who that candidate would be. The Yes's received only 45% of the vote. As a result, Chile's first multicandidate election since 1970 was held in 1989.

It could hardly be called a victory for democracy. The upper house, the Senate, continued to be packed with military appointees. The secret police and the military remained protected by amnesty. The military budget—a major burden on the Chilean economy, remained autonomous and untouchable.

The excesses of military rule persisted in Chile for a further ten years. Torturers were elected to office, and the social security system and public schools remained privatized. In the decade leading up to 1998, real salaries declined by 10% and were still 10% lower than during the Allende period.

2016. Looking Ahead

What does the future hold? A neighbor of mine, one who has read a book or two, suggests that events will follow the pattern Chile followed from 1971 to 1988. Ultimately, military rule will yield to civilian with the restoration of Congress and an elected president but on the same conditions that were negotiated by the Pinochot government: No prosecutions for past misdeeds and the top army officers to form a new Senate, appointed, not elected, unlike the old Senate, but with all the old legislative body's powers.

Arguing in favor of this scenario is that military leadership has seldom been an economic success story. In the words of David Steinberg writing in regard to Burma/Myanmar, "The military command structure permeated decision making, so that when orders were given that even common sense would have indicated could not succeed, they had to be obeyed and somehow tortuously justified." Of course, the same was true in regard to the USSR's many failed 5-year plans and China's Cultural Revolution, the disastrous results of their communist command structure. Slavish following of a leader's top-down orders was responsible for the total or near total-failures of such capitalistic enterprises as Xerox, GM, and Toyota. In Chile under military rule in the 1970's the wholesale adoption of American economist Milton Friedman's "social market economy" led to immediate declines in production and consumer buying power and a decline in employment. Readoption of these same failed policies by the neoconservative Bush administration in the first decade of the new century led to precisely the same result.

Although our present military government has chosen to follow much the same economic course, I think this scenario is unlikely. In contrast to Chile's military rule, which was dominated by one man from the outset, our military rulers are more dispersed, in geography as well as philosophy. The Navy has taken up residence on the West Coast, the Air Force the Mountain States, and the Army, the South. New England, the Midwest, and the Mid-Atlantic States have all come under different fiefdoms. Perhaps, in time, one leader may come to dominate, after which my neighbor's scenario becomes a long-term possibility. I think it more likely that our nation will be ripped apart, and our States, no longer united will be broken up into principalities, each to go its separate way. Of course, this separation too is an illusion, for whether a military or civilian government rules in an area, the multi-national corporations will continue to wield all the power.

The "national news" as reported in newspapers and on TV has gradually become regional news, at least such is the case on the West Coast where I live. The weather and crime reports (with apprehension and punishment of the suspect following quickly) are regional. Accounts of celebrities are national and national commercials (Coke, Dove, Viagra) run alongside local ones. What knowledge I have of other regions and other countries is rapidly becoming out of date, for about four months ago, cable and Internet access was restricted to regional channels.

I suspect, but can't be sure, that we have invaded Canada. Last week, I purchased a train ticket from LA to Vancouver, thinking I might visit my relatives. Appended to my e-ticket was a note that an exit visa would no longer be required. (It's good that I prefer trains; the cost of civilian air travel has risen dramatically and all west-east travel is highly restricted.)

The border to Mexico is still closed in both directions. I suspect our Government has no desire to invade countries whose citizens would cost more to support than they are likely to contribute. (Unlike Nazi Germany, we do not yet visualize ourselves as a master race.) Laborers are brought across the border to work on our harvests, but they are required to return to their homelands and growers who cannot account for all their workers at the end of a season will be fined. China (at least as of four months ago) has found itself similarly restricted. Invading the arable lands of Laos and Cambodia would only burden them with a poverty-stricken hungry population as their takeover of the Northern Korean Peninsula amply demonstrated.

One possible scenario sees a near-term invasion of the western United States by China. Apparently, one of their submarines was detected in the coastal waters off Northern California and was as quickly torpedoed. Since then the Navy has laid claim to all the waters up to 200 miles off our shores. These probes on China's part may or may not have continued; they may be real or feigned, designed by the authorities to keep our citizenry in a state of compliance. I understand that the situation is (or was as I am four months behind) much worse on the east coast.

Another less likely possibility stems from the rumors, one hears of a desire for democracy among the military rank and file, a possibility which must be offset against the reality I viewed following a Lakers game in Inglewood of a company of Marines setting a neighbor afire, shooting many of those who tried to flee, then carting off the female survivors for some other purpose.

So these are our prospects:

1. A continuation of military rule for an indefinite period (one sure to extend beyond my lifetime) with a continually widening gap between rich and poor. Senior citizens like myself already have seen our benefits remain fixed in the face of rising prices, while adequate medical care has become less and less available. Education is privatized or limited to military personnel and upward mobility outside the military will become less and less likely with each succeeding generation.

2. Open warfare among the various independent regions of the former United States and Canada followed by a possible invasion from abroad.

A third very unlikely possibility, visualized in the last century by the science fiction writer Damon Knight, is the division of our country into regions whose citizens are bound to one or the other of the great multinational keiretsu such as Coke-Proctor Gamble or Kraft-Phillip Morris-GM.

Acknowledgements

Although much of this work is fictional, representing reasoned extrapolation on my part, it is based on a solid core of fact including such texts as

Nemesis: The Last Days of the American Republic by Chalmers A. Johnson (Metropolitan Books, 2007)

See No Evil: The True Story of a Ground Soldier in the CIA's War on Terrorism by Robert Baer (Crown, 2002)

Burma/Myanmar: What Everyone Needs to Know by David I. Steinberg (Oxford University Press, USA, 2009)

The Condor Years: How Pinochet and His Allies Brought Terrorism to Three Continents by John Dinges (New Press, 2004)

Uruguay in Transition: From Civilian to Military Rule by Edy Kaufman (Transaction Books, 1979)

Dude, Where's My Country? by Michael Moore (Thorndike Press, 2004)

The Shock Doctrine: The Rise of Disaster Capitalism, by Naomi Klein (Metropolitan Books, 2007)

Lies My Teacher Told Me: Everything Your American History Textbook Got Wrong by James W Loen (New Press, 1995, 2007).

Pinochet and me, by marc cooper (Verso, 2001)

Part II. The
. Basis for our Predictions

Prolog

In the previous section, we argued that the demonstrations and counter-demonstrations occasioned by a disastrous economy would lead inevitably to a military take-over. We couldn't have been more wrong. Already, the armed services have control over more than 75% of the Federal budget and one of the current Presidential candidates is promising to provide trillions more if elected. A takeover would only give the military additional responsibility without further remuneration. This book is devoted to exploring the events of the past sixty plus years that led to the military's dominance of our once democratic country.

We argue that since World War II our military has focused on its own expansion at the expense of its effectiveness. The numbers of those of general and flag rank, no longer subject to trial by fire, have grown beyond all need. Their perks have increased dramatically while their responsibilities to those who serve under them have decreased. We will show that the military-industrial establishment has been egged on in its growth by a legislature that is completely under the influence both of large multi-national corporations and of other nations. And that the mistakes made in past wars have never been corrected.

We begin with a reappraisal of our original forecast and follow with an analysis of the successive U.S. military incursions since World War II. We'll document the many subtle changes whereby the quality of our armed services has deteriorated even as its size became an ever greater drain on the US economy. We'll reexamine the changes that occurred during the Korean Conflict, the Vietnam War, our interventions in South American and Central American affairs, the first and second Oil Wars, the ill-fated invasion of Afghanistan, and conclude with our prospects in the ongoing and losing struggle with Communist China.

As an afterthought we offer suggestions as to what might be done to slow the downward progress of our once great nation, albeit with little hope that any of our suggestions will be implemented in time.

Prequel

It was the spring of 2007 when I first realized that a military takeover in America was inevitable. Not that we weren't already halfway there. As early as the mid-fifties, Eisenhower had prophesized that the military-industrial complex would swallow our economy. Reading Chalmers Johnson' _Nemesis_ a half-century later, I was to learn that the U.S. Air force had set up golf courses (with an adjoining air base as cover) in more than 90 countries. I learned that the U.S. Army was Coca-Cola's biggest customer as well as Procter and Gamble's biggest customer, to say nothing of the many manufacturers from whom the military acquire weapons, armored vehicles, planes, missiles, ships and other military equipment.

The media also is the military's beneficiary. Other branches of government might have to be allotted pro bono public service announcements. The military paid for their commercials. The Marines even sponsored NBA games.

Our Defense Department purchases and uses more gasoline than any other customer and is the principal source of revenue for the Saudis. Billions each day were spent in Iraq and are being spent in Afghanistan, for troop movements require huge amounts of high-grade gasoline. (As do unnecessary flights by Air Force officers who wish to receive flight pay.)

The general officers live high off the hog: A five-bedroom residence, across the street from the famed Biltmore Golf Course, is provided rent-free to Marine Gen. John F. Kelly as head of U.S. Southern Command, which oversees military operations in the Caribbean Latin America. It costs the taxpayer $160,000 a year, plus $402,000 for renovations and security improvements now underway.

When Obama failed to live up to even a fraction of his promises, I was disillusioned, frustrated and angry along with millions of other voters. What I failed to realize was that the office of President in the United States is like that of the Queens of Britain and the Netherlands, strictly for appearances. Our marching orders come from the heads of the armed services.

We did not get out of Iran as scheduled; instead, we invaded Afghanistan for the second time, a move which spelled disaster for our economy as it had for the lives and the livelihoods of Afghanistan's dozen and a half other invaders throughout history beginning with Tamerlane. (Genghis Khan was smart; he went around that mountainous country and captured everything else his troops could reach). Obama promised we would leave Cuba, a country whose land we'd occupied as far back as the Spanish-American war two centuries ago—but no, we did not do that either.

Have he and his family been threatened? Or blackmailed into doing the dirty? The first explanation seems most reasonable as the military has thousands of trained assassins on call. To say nothing of the six-years' worth of torturers the Bush administration trained at Guantanamo.

The true explanation of our successive invasions of Afghanistan and Iraq has remained elusive, though dozens of proposals abound. No weapons of mass destruction were found on invading Iraq, nor had anyone who read the newspapers (and remembered what was written there) expected to find them. While I knew that the so-called justifications for our invasion of Iraq were lies, had known almost the moment they left Bush's lips, 35% of Americans still swear by their tattered legitimacy. As Robert Baer, a former CIA agent, reported in his book, *See No Evil,* Saddam had sold off all the weapons the first President Bush had given him to the Moslem Brotherhood within weeks of their receipt. As for the official pretext for invading Afghanistan to capture Osama bin Laden; somehow, despite the elderly bin Laden's being a late stage diabetic suffering from kidney failure so that he was in constant need of dialysis, we succeeded in finding him only after an eleven-year search and then it was in a different country altogether.

The "alternative" explanations were equally suspect: We invaded Iraq so that Bush Jr. could rebuild Bush Sr.'s legacy and not incidentally, get his approval ratings back up. The Taliban having destroyed so many of the poppy fields, our invasion of Afghanistan was only to get the heroin back on the streets. This latter rationale must be given some credence for indeed the heroin did return to our streets in quantity and when the Taliban needed money to finance their cause, they'd no choice but to encourage poppy cultivation.

The fact remains that whatever these many wars' true rationale, their end result was to further expand the military's power and to further shift our nation's wealth from the hands of the many to the hands of the few. In the pages that follow, I shall try to trace the inevitability of the takeover and to trace its progress to date.

The Prime Causes

If asked to name the reasons why a country, that throughout its entire history had provided a beacon of religious and political freedom for the balance of the world, should yield to a military dictatorship, albeit one that rules solely from behind the scenes, a single phrase leaps to mind:

It's the economy stupid.

We've all heard the story of the 26-year-old who back in 2010 had to suspend her photography and sculpture career because her parents could no longer support her. "My artistic career is put on the side because I have to make a living."

But focusing on a single cause for our tragedy would be misleading. True, the sharp decline into bankruptcy that accompanied the Bush administration's neo-conservative policies is among the chief reasons democracy is failing in America, accompanied as it is by a lack of civilian jobs, an abrupt decline in personal income, and the feeling that we were somehow second rate as individuals and as a nation.

Still, this is not the first depression our country has experienced. Nor is it the first in which the very wealthy behave in flagrant disregard of the needs of the middle class. But it is the first in which those most responsible for bringing about the system's failure were able to run an extensive and successful program of disinformation.

We are told by the right wing to worry about welfare fraud, though the fraud perpetrated by those who received military contracts in Iraq and to rebuild domestically after Hurricane Katrina was a thousand times greater. We are told to rage over taxes, though by abolishing the estate tax, we are perpetuating the ranks of the privileged at the expense of the middle class.

Some of us have gone without work for several years, (and, in consequence, are no longer included in the employment statistics published by the Labor Department) have lost our homes, and our health insurance, yet our taxpayer money is used not to create jobs, but to bail out a dozen failed banks whose officers subsequently receive bonuses of fifty million dollars or more apiece! Fifty million! Fifty dollars would have meant another month of cable for a family or a meal at a good restaurant to raise the flagging spirits of a man and his wife. Five hundred would have covered my monthly mortgage, while five thousand per month was required for the mortgages of the many who'd been tempted in the previous five years to buy beyond their means. Fifty million could have made the payments on 10,000 mortgages, kept 10,000 families in their homes!

In September 2012, it became evident that only a second job-creation program similar to that Roosevelt put into place in the 1930s would succeed in priming the pump (as well as repairing our rapidly-decaying infrastructure). Instead, the decision was made to bail out the bankers and the Chinese government, which held most of our paper, by spending 40 million dollars a month in purchasing worthless mortgage-backed securities.

Congress has always been corrupt, as witness Mark Twain's acerbic comments on the 19th Century version of that august body. But never before has its members, suppositories all jammed firmly up the assholes of the multinational corporations, been quite so shameless, so indifferent to the needs or the opinions of their constituents.

Congressmen's votes could be and traditionally were purchased by big-money interests. But from the founding of the American Republic to the middle of the 20th century, these were our own American-born interests, or own multi-millionaires. Beginning in the 1950's, as an adjunct to Marshall Aid, Congress began to get on the payroll of foreign nations. Today, our elected representatives are the beneficiaries of multi-national corporations, foreign governments, and individuals who bear little or no loyalty to the U.S.A. electorate.

90% of the wealth of the Republican Party's candidate in the 2012 elections is located abroad. Where can his loyalties lie?

Today, foreign interests are permitted to own and operate our domestic media— newspapers, TV stations, and radio. And as we will see later in this chapter, China has taken full advantage of this loophole.

From 2008 through 2010, layoffs by and closures of

our domestic corporations continued for more than two years until 15% of the population was unemployed (25% if we exclude the military from these calculations), yet the number of foreign workers admitted legally was permitted to double. From the few point of their multi-national corporate employers, these foreign workers were a bonus. Skilled workers in the main, they were willing to labor for half the wages our native-born engineers, programmers, professors and other professionals had grown accustomed to.

Work was to be had, the right-wing media critics declared, if only one looked hard enough. Work at McDonalds or some other fast-food restaurant? Not if one couldn't speak the language, couldn't relate to one's illegal coworkers. For at the behest of the corporations, illegals poured across our porous borders, and enforcement of the laws against their employment was rare indeed. In the month of September 2012, with hundreds of thousands of native Californians still without work, a bill in the California legislature would give work permits to illegal immigrants. During the same month, 72,000 illegal immigrants were permitted to apply for work permits under a new Federal program.

Given the engagement of Abraham Lincoln's administration in a war he did not want, he'd felt he had no choice but to institute a tax on incomes. This tax would be graduated according to the taxpayer's income, for, as Lincoln put it, those who gained the most from this country and its wars ought to pay the most for its support.

A century and a half later, in a parody of basic economics, Bush Lite launched a series of wars our nation did not need and proposed to pay for them by reducing the taxes on the rich. The not unexpected result was a deeper deficit and economic ruin for our nation.

Why did we not protest? The ruling Romans used circuses to divert their populace. Our ruling classes offer Jerry Springer, Fox News, and Reality TV.

Terry Gilliam's film *Brazil* proved prophetic as we found ourselves threatened daily with terrorist attacks. Bush's newly appointed Homeland Security Tsar sounded a series of red, yellow, and orange alerts. Civil liberty was sacrificed to survival.

Let's take another closer look at the differences and similarities between then and the now of 2012.

1. **Establishment of a Military-Industrial Complex**. During World War II, the manufacturers of weapons and military equipment had seen immense profits. They were never to forgo such profits again. Our isolationist right suddenly developed a strong interest in foreign affairs. Our troops went to Korea, then to Vietnam, then to Columbia and Iraq. As the 20th century ended and peace was finally in our grasp, we enlarged our army and sent our troops—with inferior and often inappropriate arms and equipment, into the Middle East. Under

Bush, it was decreed that we would purchase weapons without testing them.

2. **Failure to thin the numbers of those of General and Flag rank**. In World War II, there was one officer to every ten enlisted men. During World War II, senior American commanders were given at best a few months in which to succeed or be replaced. "In the latter part of the Korean War and in our wars in Vietnam, Afghanistan, and Iraq, relief of generals by generals became all but extinct," writes Thomas E. Ricks in The Generals. By the end of March 2010, the 1.4 million service members on active duty were being led by 950 generals and flags— or one for every 1,489 troops.

3. **Rise of the Right Wing**. Curiously our entry into the war in 1941 was never assured. Powerful right wing forces (encouraged and often subsidized by Germany) were at work to forestall our entry. The novel, *Fatherland,* depicts a mythical future in which Joseph Kennedy became President in 1940 and kept America neutral. The attacks on Roosevelt at that time are echoed in their ferocity by the attacks on Obama today (encouraged and often subsidized by China). The big distinction in the decades is

4. **Centralized Media**. In the olden days, our media was decentralized. The Media was partisan then as now, but as it was in the hands of hundreds of individuals with half a dozen newspapers and a dozen independently owned TV and radio stations in each major market, hundreds of points of view could be and were expressed. Today, our media is national rather than regional in scope. As it costs far more to insert a story in a national medium than in a local paper and few but the very rich can afford it. Moreover, foreign interests can and do purchase time on our airwaves. One country, China, owns a TV/radio/and newspaper network Fox, outright.

5. **The Dumbing Down of Education**. In the 19th and early 20th century, even elementary school students were fully aware of the crises that had given rise to our nation. Our ancestors, they learned, had come to America from Europe seeking religious freedom. For in England and throughout Western Europe in the 17th and 18th Centuries, the major religions—Anglicans, Catholics, Lutherans, Puritans and Presbyterians had in common a fervent desire to see the members of all other religions tortured, imprisoned and put to death. America's founding fathers resolved that hatred would be put aside, religious freedom and freedom of speech

guaranteed. To the rest of the world we became a beacon of intellectual and religious liberty. Today, our students may remain aware that we are or once were such a beacon, but are no longer told why. (Check the state of your own knowledge via *Lies My Teacher Told Me* by James Lowen.)

6. **Guns.** One non-factor in the acceptance of the takeover, though one often favored by psychologists, is the prevalence of guns in civilian hands. In 2004 alone, 29,569 American civilians died by gunfire: 16,750 in firearm suicides, 11,935 in firearm homicides, 649 in unintentional shootings, and 235 in firearm deaths of unknown intent, according to the National Center for Health Statistics. More than twice this number are treated in emergency rooms each year for nonfatal firearm injuries.

   Yet the rate of firearms mortality peeked in the 1970's and has actually declined by one-third since that time. The percentage of American households that report having any guns in the home dropped nearly 20 percentage points from a high of 54 percent in 1977 to 34.5 percent in 2006.

   A psychological factor that may well have desensitized us to violence is our long exposure to mayhem and gun play, real as well as fictional, via the television and other news media. No public outcry arose against our use of torture against enemy combatants during the unending war in Iraq and it was but a small further step toward our acceptance of the use of torture today against those the government labels as "the enemies amongst us." (Our torturers are highly skilled. Latin America has looked to us for instruction since the 1970's. And during the Bush II administration we raised a bumper crop of our own in Guantanamo Bay.)

7. **China and our policy of unilateral free trade**. Perhaps the act most destructive to US interests that Nixon committed during his Presidency was to open the door to China. That grandiose half-wit was completely outsmarted for the door proved to open in one direction only: China-made goods poured into the U.S. at bargain prices, putting many of our companies out of business and a multitude of our workers out of jobs. The U.S. gained nothing in return; neither our advice nor our goods and services were wanted. How could China make goods so cheaply? By using convicts and members of their army, practices our own country outlawed.

They invest heavily in U.S. securities and are among the United States' major creditors. They hold more U.S. bonds than any other bond holder. The costly bank bailouts of 2008 and 2009 were largely the result of pressure from the Chinese.

President Roosevelt brought the United States out of a major depression in the 1930's, creating hundreds of thousands of jobs through direct government spending on rebuilding America's infrastructure. Although today, hundreds of thousands remain unemployed and our infrastructure today cries out for repair--we need to fill in potholes, replace worn sewer pipes, clean the drinking water supply, and build high speed rail lines, under pressure from the Chinese, the Obama administration chose to shore up the prices of mortgage-backed securities (to the tune of $40 billion a month) thus rewarding both foreign investors and our far-from-in-need financial community.

Taking the role the CIA played in South America's military takeovers of the 1970's are both China's Communist-controlled civilian spy agency MSS, the Ministry of State Security, and its military counterpart, the Second Department of the People's Liberation Army, or 2PLA.

These two as well as other branches of China's government also exercise a more direct role. They bribe Congressmen and presidential advisers. A costly stimulus package of $300 per person during the Bush administration led to dramatic increases in the sale of Chinese made goods, while sales of heavy equipment made in the USA remained flat or stalled completely.

In 1999, as a result of Rupert Murdoch's marriage to Chinese-born Deng Wendi, Fox News and other Murdoch-dominated media in the U.S. and abroad took an even more dramatic turn to the right. The objective from China's point of view was to destabilize the American government. For as long as America remained a democracy, there would always be pressure on the Chinese government to relax its own dictatorial policies. Not incidentally, the role of the MSS is also to bolster Beijing's Communist Party rule by repressing religious and political dissent. The steady flow of disinformation emanating from the Murdoch Empire serves this end well as witness the run-up and the sequel to the 2012 elections.

The Tea Party, heavily subsidized by our own multi-millionaires, has pressed heavily for the government to take a reduced role, to cut back essential services even those with a direct impact on our country's defense. The virtual abandonment of inspections of cargo from abroad under the Bush and Obama administrations permits the importation of dangerous and defective goods from China. Are there weapons of mass destruction hidden amid the cartons of plastic toys? As a result of the cutbacks in essential service, the American public no longer have any way to knowing. We send our troops abroad while leaving our borders undefended. As for those goods that are actually declared on the importers' manifests, the long terms effects on the health and economy of our people, as in the case of toxic wallboard, are just beginning to be felt.

The ultimate future of Chimerica , so named by Michael J, Casey author of <u>The Unfair Trade</u>, is a massive leveling of incomes as those of China's lower classes rise while those of our lower and middle classes fall, with the military the hidden ruler in both countries.

8.   **The Magic Pill**. The efforts of French bacteriologists in the 1920's led to the near eradication of tuberculosis in Japan, Eastern Europe, and France, a literal gift to the poor. Dr. Albert Sabin, a Jewish Polish-American, aided by the Russian government, developed the oral vaccine that has led to the near eradication of polio. (Curiously, through the extensive public-relations efforts of the March of Dimes purchased with the tax-free donations they'd received from Americans, we were led to believe that the research of Jonas Salk the March of Dimes had sponsored led to the cure, when in fact the Salk vaccine gave polio and leukemia to

thousands. This would not be the last time in America that public relations efforts would successfully place a positive spin on disaster, as the administrations of Nixon, Reagan, and Bush soon revealed.)

But it was the efforts of chemists at Syntex and Searle that were to totally revolutionize the American way of life and set the stage for our present predicament. The pill put women in charge of their lives. Smaller families were the immediate result. No longer would a woman be obliged to bear children until the male parent had a male heir.

Smaller families meant that post-pill children had greater attention lavished upon them and grew up with a sense of privilege and entitlement. In former times, the oldest child would have been forced to move out of the family home to make room for his younger still-growing siblings. Now he or she was permitted to stay still living off the family dole. Or, if he or she left, she would be permitted to return after first trying out life in the cruel world. These post-pill children became our boomerang generation. All had in common the expectation that their government, taking the place of their parents, would continue to offer extensive benefits at no cost to them. Uncivil discourse, the threat as well as the actuality of violence our society experienced throughout 2010 were merely a symptom, not a cause. Our grownup children want benefits without taxation and are encouraged in this naive desire by the very rich who, not incidentally, own all the major media.

Curiously, a half-century earlier, it was the far right wing in the form of the John Burch Society that had plastered billboards all over the Southern United States, with a portrait of Uncle Sam and a legend reading, "He's not your father, he's your uncle."

On a Picnic Morning

Writing in _This Kind of War_, T.R. Fehrenback noted that the Korean conflict (June 1950 to July 1953) was the first war in which company and battalion commanders were denied the opportunity to learn from their mistakes. All combat decisions were made for them by general officers dictating from a remote location in Japan far from the battlefield.

The result, Fehrenback predicted and the Vietnam War soon verified, would be a new generation of general officers utterly lacking in the combat experience that is essential to making area-wide decisions.

The Korean conflict also provided three other lessons to only one of which the U.S. took much heed. First, the American soldier's chief concern was his own comfort-- his country's future came a distant second. Some effort was put into correcting this, albeit the result was to generate among the average American soldier a universal contempt for all non-white and non-black Americans, allies as well as enemies.

Second, officers out of touch with combat conditions are bound to make poor decisions. For example, Macarthur wanted to use nuclear weapons in North Korea. Yet, the fallout would have affected all Koreans, not just those in the target area, south as well as north, democratic as well as communist, along with their U.S. and U.N. allies in the field.

Third, the far-from industrialized Chinese, just emerging from their own civil war were not merely an unexpected but a formidable opponent. Strong enough that the allies were forced to settle at the end of the conflict for a return to pre-war boundaries.

A half-century later, China is the dominant military power in the world, yet Congress, the American public, and, seemingly, the American military remain focused on Russia, Iran, and North Korea, everywhere but on the real enemy. In his speech to the 2012 Republican convention, Romney chided Obama for ignoring Russia and the members of the so-called Axis of Evil, but said not one word about the Chinese menace.

The explanation is straightforward. Our officers and politicians have sold out. The U.S. offers no bar to foreign investment, whether in its media or its Congressmen. And the Chinese have invested wisely. Today, thirty-five percent of all Americans get all their news from a media outlet owned by the PLA2, the intelligence wing of the Chinese Peoples' Liberation Army.

One other peculiarity of the Korean Conflict should be mentioned, one that will play a pivotal role in the balance of this text. The U.S. military does not fight to win.

Throughout the Korean Conflict, the United States made no attempt to bomb North Korea, not even after the massed armies of the Chinese arrived, even though we had clear air superiority.[1] Instead, we were content to

---

[1] In fairness to our military, they did recommend the U.S.

slog it out on the ground, where, given the sheer numbers of the enemy, particularly after the Chinese arrived, we had no hope of winning. Winning, it appeared, was no longer what the U.S is about. And when the inevitable Chinese vs. U.S. conflict breaks out once again on the Korean Peninsula or the South-China Sea, this time the two sides will have comparably sized and equipped air force and navies, and America will have no hope whatever of winning.

---

provide air support, but were denied its use by President Truman who feared the still-badly decimated Russians would take advantage of the diversion of our troops to Asia by attacking in Europe. Instead, the Russians, showing no such restraint, provided air cover for the attacking Chinese.

I Started a Joke

"I'm convinced that no military victory is possible in that kind of theater."
"As long as I am president we will not go in with ground troops into Vietnam."

Dwight Eisenhower, 1951, 1954

Reminiscing about our war in Vietnam raises many questions, not the least of which is "why were we there?" Why did we invade a country from which both the French and the Chinese Communists already had retreated? Did we have a secret plan?

(One might have similar qualms about our invasion of and continued preoccupation with Afghanistan, a country that two men, Genghis Khan and Alexander the Great, who had in their day conquered most of the then-known world, chose to bypass, and two other countries, Britain --once—and Russia—twice— had driven themselves to the brink of bankruptcy in the course of abortive invasions.)

Why did we ignore the advice of Bernard Fell who argued in his many books (see, for example, _The Two Vietnams_), correctly, that Vietnam was not one but many nations, united as a country only in the minds of European geographers? Why did we back a notoriously corrupt government?" (Oops, didn't mean to bring up Afghanistan a second time.) Why did we continue to fight the last wars, in which the ground troops of two nations faced off, instead of stressing counterinsurgency tactics? [2] Firepower--$9.3 billion for an air campaign in one fiscal year--was all General Westmoreland could come up with. And, as Lt. Col. Herbert asks in his book, *Soldier*, "Why did we not make use of modern technology?"

Herbert was referring to the infrared scopes we had and the North Vietnamese did not. The night belonged to us, yet our officers chose to quit at dusk, much in the way British Officers of the 18th through 19th centuries would knock off fighting in time for tea.

The United States also failed to employ our night-time technology in Afghanistan. As a result, the Taliban succeed in penetrating Camp Bastion via a night-time incursion in September 2012.

Did we win in Vietnam?

Without a clear statement of goals in advance of declaring war, it is impossible to win or lose. If one Googles or Yahoos "goals Vietnam War" some forty years later, one gets a series of vague answers, such as "to stop communism." The same is true if one Yahoos "goals Korean War."

Goals must be spelled out on the political level before the military is asked to send troops and material abroad. Before the troops are sent, the armed services need to have in hand clear cut plans of attack.

---

[2] To be fair, the Marine Corp, led by Lt. Gen. Victor Krulak, did launch a successful campaign by working in concert with Vietnamese villagers, at least until the Army called them off.

All this assumes that the nation endorses the proposed war and the military have been given a clear go-ahead by the political establishment. The exception arises as it has in the 21st Century when the military are the political establishment.

Only in recent years have Americans shown much desire for war. Regardless of what you may have gleaned from books and movies about the War Between the States, only a few Americans participated and, in the war's initial stages, did so reluctantly for periods that were too short to be effective.

A very small number of Americans served in World War I (and only in that war's last stages. In part, this was because there was little agreement within America as to which side of "the European War" was right and which was wrong.

World War II was much less ambiguous; those who served in the U.S. military in World War II have never questioned what they did was right. Yet America as a nation entered that war only with the greatest reluctance and only when we had been attacked on our own soil by Japan.

Given the subsequent debacle in Korea, this explains why America's entry into Vietnam was done with a minimum of fanfare, with advisors rather than with troops and in a highly tentative fashion. The 2000 men dispatched to Vietnam in 1961 had increased to only 16,500 by 1964. In 1961, few Americans knew or cared that we were fighting a war there. But by March 1965 the

U.S was able to begin bombing North Vietnam with strong public support.

Larger and larger numbers of men were sent abroad subsequently, so that by the end of 1995 more than 200,000 American troops were in South Vietnam. Even so, the initial role of the military was to be a limited one. They were instructed that their role in the conflict was to be purely defensive in nature. Second, they were only to act in support of the government of the South. As Fell notes, this notoriously corrupt government represented only a fraction of the multiple peoples who live in South Vietnam.

The military blundered in Vietnam in at least four ways. They did not take advantage of any of the following:

- Their lead in technology.
- The power structure of the country. Vietnam was predominantly tribal in nature, the power structure residing in a multitude of village headmen, rather than in a central government. Instead, they chose to behave as if Vietnam were a dictatorship.
- The experience of their fighting men. The initial tour of duty for American service men in Vietnam was limited to one year. Those who learned and survived were then sent home. Worse, officers were rotated every six months just as they began to learn their jobs and gain the trust of their men. Logic dictated

these officers keep their heads down, avoid risk, and call on the artillery and air force to do a job that was really the infantry's. This approach was spectacularly unsuccessful against an enemy familiar with the terrain who could slip away quickly.

- Their gains. Bluntly, too much of their troop's time was spent in hold-fast mode. Idle hands do make the devil's handiwork. Assassinating an unpopular commanding officer goes back many centuries to at least 1704 at the Battle of Blenheim, if not to when the Roman Legion occupied Britain. But Vietnam witnessed such a large number of assaults that "fragging" became part of the American vernacular.
- Americans sentimentality. We've all seen in movies, how our heroes would leave no bodies behind. But when this cinematic behavior was imitated by troops in Viet Nam, the Viet Cong would kill the rest of the body-laden group.

A further major failure to be repeated years later in both Iraq and Afghanistan was the high command's neglect of the civilian population. With the high command's emphasis on destroying the enemy, collateral damage was inevitable. Vietnamese civilians who might have proven invaluable allies (if only as eyes and ears) were driven into the arms of the Viet Cong to seek protection instead.

Did the military learn from its mistakes? Not one bit. Army doctrine continues to emphasize army against army much as the redcoats had persisted in using against American irregulars in 1776. Counterinsurgency tactics were seldom used in Iraq and are seldom used in Afghanistan today.

Fragging persists. An American army captain and his 1st lieutenant were killed in 2005 in Iraq by a claymore mine placed in the Captain's office window. Idle hands generated the incidents that so turned the Afghan people against their American liberators including Koran burnings, urinating on corpses, and the deliberate murder of women and children.

Nor did the politicians learn. The Vietnam War launched the U.S. on its first step toward bankruptcy and total dependence on the financial maneuvers of the Chinese Communist party. To pay for the war, Nixon took America off the gold standard so he could print an unlimited amount of currency.

In a Time of Peace?

Though the late 1970's and the 1980's were a time of relative peace, at least for Americans, the American military continued to expand its presence throughout the world, an expansion that has persisted to the present day.

Sixty-seven years after the end of WW II, the U.S. still has a substantial military presence in Japan (or, rather, in the adjoining island of Okinawa). It maintains several divisions in Korea, to say nothing of Guantanamo Bay in Cuba, which it first occupied in 1898. While the United States no longer occupies the Philippines which they invaded at the end of the 19th century, they still maintained a large number of air and naval bases there up until 1992.

The trend continued into the 1990's. With the collapse of the Soviet Union, the United States was quick to bribe their way into military bases in the newly-formed Central Asian republics. The result has been a steady drain on the American economy both for the annual "rent" for the bases and for the salaries of the troops stationed there, while the "rents" have propped up a series of dictatorships in the region.

The debacles of the Korean and Vietnam Wars were only the first of American's missteps toward the dissolution of democracy. Most of the 1970s and 1980s were devoted to terrorizing the people of Latin and Central America.

Our attacks on their civilian population began on the 11th of September, 1973 with the U.S supporting a military coup against the lawfully-elected President of Chile. Next, we were to supply torturers and trainers to the despotic military rulers of Argentina and Brazil.

During President Regan's administration, American arms and advisors went to Nicaragua and Guatemala to help their dictatorial regimes suppress all opposition.

The 1980's also saw the US arming both sides in the lengthy Iran-Iraq war from September 1980 to August 1988. The war began in the air, with Iraq fielding Russian-made aircraft and the Iranians (with whom the US no longer had diplomatic relations) flying US-manufactured aircraft. As the war progressed, the U.S. soon began supplying both intelligence and materiel to the Iraqis along with the pesticides and poisons they needed to make chemical weapons. Then, business being business, the U.S. began supplying weapons to the Iranians as well.

Dying for the House of Saud

The assent of the first President Bush marked a dramatic change in American foreign policy. The United States began loaning out its armies much like the Hessians of old to do the bidding of Saudi Arabia. (Of course, they continued to provide back-door assistance to Latin and Central American dictatorships.)

Big Oil didn't object; the military didn't object—wars are essential to the retention of otherwise redundant officers of general and flag rank; and the weapons manufacturers could only applaud. As ten times the number of necessary bombs were dropped on Baghdad at the start of the first Gulf War(to be watched live on CNN by enthralled Americans as if the bombs were only fireworks and the lives lost were those of Hollywood stunt men who would simply pick themselves up once the cameras moved on). Although the first Gulf War lasted only six months, 88.500 tons of bombs were dropped, almost all on military targets. Not a problem; orders to their manufacturers' for the bombs' replacements were quickly dispatched by the Pentagon. (Curiously, many of the Pentagon's procurement agents were hired subsequently by the weapon makers.

As anyone familiar with the operettas of Gilbert and Sullivan is aware, politics has always been an essential component of the military life: "I polished up that handle so carefully, that now I am the Ruler of the Queen's

Navy." As shall be discussed subsequently, in today's military, one must heed not only one's superiors but the ones their superiors serve, regretfully, not all of whom are Americans or have America's best interests at heart.

On the plus side, the first oil war achieved its objectives and became the only American military action since World War II to do so. This came about for three reasons:

- The objectives of this war were well well-defined, specifically to force Saddam Hussein to withdraw Iraqi troops from Kuwait.
- Sufficient men and materiel were provided from the onset to achieve this declared objective. The military buildup of 543,000 troops (twice the number used in the 2003 invasion of Iraq) was still only 73% of the coalitions combined forces.
- When the objective was achieved, the United States withdrew from the field. (A move made necessary in part by the need to leave Iraq as a buffer against an equally militant Iran.)

The first oil war was preceded by extensive diplomatic negotiations. Negotiation is the art of the possible. The first oil war might have been avoided entirely, had Iraq retreated from Kuwait. The pretexts on which the United States was to invade Iraq a second time as well as Afghanistan in the next century were preceded by impossible demands that the enemy was in no position to fulfill.

Afghanistan I: The Failed Pursuit of Bin Laden

In 2001, after a group of Saudis attacked the Trade Center, the United States invaded Afghanistan in pursuit of Osama Bin Laden, the attack's mastermind. Although Bin Laden was burdened by dialysis equipment, he succeeded in evading the Americans and slipping across the border into Pakistan. Blame for the failed pursuit can be laid on the commander of the U.S. Forces, Tommy R. Franks. Franks was a product of the attack first, think second school of thought in which most of the current surviving generation of senior general officers received their training. He made no attempt to surround the arch-criminal, but focused instead on a bombing campaign (against who or what was never made clear). Such an approach had failed in Viet Nam, and, not surprisingly, it failed in Afghanistan, too.

Iraq II: A Failure of Leadership

"How can you tell when GWBush is lying?"
"His mouth is open."

More spies from more nations are at work in the United States than in any other country. The reasons are two-fold.

1. The United States is rich in technology so spies are drawn to us in their search for industrial and military data.
2. Our heterogeneous population and porous borders make us easy to penetrate.

A white face would stand out in China, but the Chinese have been an integral (even if a once-despised) part of the U.S. population for more than a century. By encouraging the importation (legal and illegal) of cheap labor, the United States makes it easy for the spies of all nations to sneak across our borders. Inspection of those caught sneaking in to the United States from Mexico (and those caught are but a relatively small fraction of those who make the attempt) reveals that ten percent are of Arabic, Chinese, Iranian, or other origin.

In early 2001, members of the Saudi Arabian royal family let members of the Bush family with whom they were close friends know that Saudi Arabian dissidents were organizing an attack on the United States. Over the next six months, many nations whose spies had seen the dissidents in action in the U.S., reported to the U.S. State Department privately via their embassies of what they had seen. The actions of the dissidents who would later be called terrorists were discussed in the Oval Office.

Were these warnings simply ignored? Or was an actual determination made to let the terrorist attack proceed in order to boost Bush's rapidly declining ratings? What we do know is that when FBI field agents reported that the terrorists were in the U.S. training to fly commercial aircraft, their superiors told them to stop following the terrorists. And when in August the Israelis publically reported the likely date of the attack and its likely targets, they too were ignored. (To be fair, Bush Lite, who would set a record among Presidents for vacation days in his first year of office, was on vacation for the entire month of August.)

After the attacks, then President Bush declared that he would track down those who had financed the attacks and confiscate their assets. He did not follow through. Instead, possessed with the public knowledge that the terrorists were Saudis and their organizer Bin Laden was a member of a prominent Saudi Arabian family, he declared war on Iraq!?

The real objectives of the second Gulf War were as follows:

- To boost Bush's ratings,
- To keep Iraq's oil flowing (the multinational oil companies were among Bush's biggest financial backers).

- To use up as much obsolete weaponry as possible (the weapons makers were Bush's second biggest source of campaign funds).
- To make millions of dollars for Dick Cheney and stockholders with large holdings in government contractors by allowing the contracts to proceed (or to appear to proceed) far from government oversight.
- To keep Americans employed (the U.S. economy had already soured).

These last explain why in contrast to the first Gulf war, the primary targets of the initial air campaign were civilian targets, as our air force chose to destroy electric power stations and water processing plants. It was on!

A hidden objective need also be mentioned. Among the neoconservatives, many, including President Bush, felt the President's father had betrayed the American people by pulling American troops out of Iraq before Saddam's regime had been toppled. In so thinking, they were clearly ignorant of the real reason the first President Bush (and the Saudis who financed his political campaigns) elected to withdraw troops from Iraq as quickly as possible. The elder Bush had foreseen, correctly, that only Iraq was strong enough in the Middle East to contain Iran's territorial ambitions.

How prescient the first President Bush was. How foolish his son (or, this being a democracy, how foolish those who backed his son for a second term. "Fool me once, shame on you; fool me twice, shame on me," as the saying goes.)

The neo-conservative politicians who launched Iraq II had learned a great deal from the political failures of Vietnam. They knew they needed the support of the nation in order to proceed. So they provided the nation with a series of reasons. All were lies. All were remarkably successful in harnessing public enthusiasm for the war.

- Osama bin Laden, the Saudi Arabian architect of 9/11, was hiding in Iraq. He wasn't.
- Iraq was enriching uranium. They weren't.
- Large numbers of weapons of mass destruction had been accumulated by Saddam Hussein, Iraq's dictator for use against the United States. They hadn't. While it was true that Bush's father, then Vice-President of the United States, had arranged to supply Iraq with large number of weapons of mass destruction in the late 1980's to use in its fight against Iran, according to the CIA and Robert Baer, Saddam had double-crossed the U.S. and his own people by immediately selling the weapons to the Moslem Brotherhood. The cash he received for the weapons went into his own pockets not into Iraq's treasury.

Is the American public really that gullible? Alas, the answer is yes.

Before the start of the second Gulf War, inspectors for the International Atomic Energy Agency toured Iraq and reported that they could not find the weapons. Nor, did the American armies ever find any after the invasion. Still, in 2002, the American public was led to believe in the reality of the hidden weapons of mass destruction. A decade later, a poll of Americans shows that as many as 35% still believe.

Despite initial public support for the War, the Bush administration realized, again based on the experience of President Johnson, it might quickly fade away were they to reintroduce the draft. Consequently, the initial expansion of the military was accomplished by calling up the reserves (America's weekend warriors) who many Americans secretly resented for what seemed to be collecting government money for little or no work. Next, the administration lowered the requirement for admission to the service--forget the need for a high-school diploma or passing an IQ test, and offered large enlistment bonuses. The cleansing process that General Creighton Abrams had launched in 1973 was quickly reversed. A young man or woman that might well have been a provo in Holland, or a squatter in Great Britain, or merely a layabout in another era, joined the armed services.

A third administration policy did serve to make the military more effective (while still avoiding the need for a draft) but drove many enlistees to the brink of madness.

In the 1960's, a recruit might and often did spend as little as a year in Vietnam before being rotated out. A similar limitation in the War Between the States had set back the Union war effort. But recruits in Iraq II discovered they had signed up for the duration, not only of their original contracts, but for a war that had no end in sight. Suicides, post-traumatic stress fatigue were all too common among those who served in Iraq and persist as a burden on their families today.

```
    O it's Tommy this, an' Tommy that, an'
"Tommy, go away";
But it's ``Thank you, Mister Atkins,'' when the
band begins to play,
The band begins to play, my boys, the band
begins to play,
O it's ``Thank you, Mr. Atkins,'' when the band
begins to play.
    See http://www.web-
books.com/Classics/Poetry/Anthology/Kipling/Tomm
y.htm
```

To avoid detailing the true cost of war, the Armed Services chose to cook the books. Service personnel who were injured in Iraq were quickly airlifted to another country (usually Germany) where there subsequent deaths need not be reported as casualties.

Other Bush era policies have had major consequences for today's military.

- When weapons produced under government contract failed to pass tests, the Bush government abandoned testing, nor have the tests resumed under the Obama administration.

- Our fighting forces are still-manned (or womaned) by the dregs of society who have zero tolerance for the other cultures the U.S. military allegedly serves.

You've got to know when to walk away, and when to play the game

According to Thomas E. Ricks, writing in <u>The Generals</u>, despite the occasional foray in the opposite direction , the training of officers in the American Military remains focused on tactical rather than strategic considerations: "Battalion and brigade commanders knew how to conduct a blitzkrieg, but when they became generals, they did not know what to do once that speedy attack was concluded."

After Saddam was deposed and our primary objective achieved, we should have walked away. Instead, we lingered for eight more years engaged in an unwinnable battle against both sides in a civil war that is to continue long after we leave.

Emulating the battle strategy of the redcoats during the American Revolution—and the Brits lost, you may recall—our armies waged conventional warfare when counterinsurgency tactics were called for.

Murdering and raping Iraqi civilians, failing to distinguish friend from foe, imprisoning and torturing suspects, some innocent, some guilty the army succeeded only in turning once indifferent civilians into active opponents. Yet when the horror of Abu Gharib prison came to light, no officer including the jailers' commander was court martialed or demoted.

You can't protect a people, by torturing and killing them and destroying their homes.

Yet after the expenditure of billions of dollars and thousands of lives, the three-fold result of the U.S. invasion of Iraq was:

- A weakened Iraq unable to act as a deterrent to its aggressive Shiite neighbor Iran.
- Additional suicides among returning veterans.
- The United States driven to the brink of bankruptcy, albeit a failed economy that has revealed itself only slowly since the war's end.

Why did we stay? Simply put, so that a large number of civilian contractors, all huge campaign contributors, could continue to subsist on the largess of U.S. taxpayers. As documented in Naomi Klein's The Shock Doctrine, these contractors worked for eight years, without measurable progress, on Iraq's water, power, and sewage systems. While Iraq had once boasted the finest educational system in the Middle East, our contractors soon reduced it to the status of our own urban ghetto schools.

Iraq, a creation of French and British geographers after World War I designed to secure those nations' oil rights, is home to three disparate tribal groups--Sunni, Shiites, and Kurds. Civil war ensued after our invasion and has continued after our departure. In September 2012, a year after the departure of U.S. troops had left the country, thousands of Iraqis poured into the streets to protest the actions of the United States. Civil war is guaranteed to rage there for at least the next twenty years while the Mid-East lives in increasing fear of a nuclear Iran.

The Country Alexander the Great Ignored

Strictly speaking, the U.S. invasion of Afghanistan preceded the second Iraq War. Like the latter, it replicated all the failures of previous invasions. As in the Korean Conflict, company- and battalion-level command decisions were made by high-ranking officers at a distance from the battlefield. As in the Vietnam War, the United States failed to deal with the political realities of the country they were invading, sent in an inadequate number of troops initially, and spent far too much time in holding actions when they should have been on the attack. And as was the case in the second Iraq war, they lied about the purpose of the invasion.

The summer of 2001 had been a sad one for the inhabitants of the District of Columbia as indeed it had been for the residents of most inner cities throughout the United States. A year earlier, the Taliban had put a stop to the growing of poppies and the production of opium in Afghanistan. Growers had been harassed, distributors arrested or killed. Slowly but inevitably, the supply of processed heroin that reached the United States had begun to dwindle.

By the time the summer of 2001 rolled around, the supply was only a small percentage of what it once had been. Initially, the American-based wholesalers and street dealers had been buffered from the loss, holding their profits steady by raising prices or by cutting the percentage of pure drug included in the final product.

The addicts, the dealers, and the communities they lived in experienced the pain. The addicts because they had to do without their daily fix, the communities because it took more and more burglaries to finance the purchase of what little heroin there was to be had, and the dealers and wholesalers simply because they had less to sell.

In developing countries, the wounded and the burned were given cord to bite on in place of pills, for Afghanistan had been the source of 87% of the world's opiates. By September, even the drug's importers, major contributors to the Bush campaign, had begun to fill the pinch. For them, the terrorist attacks on New York and Washington could not have come at a better time.

Within a month of the attacks, the FBI and the CIA had identified not only the terrorists—Saudis mostly—but also the source of their funds— wealthy residents of Saudi Arabia and the United Arab Emirates. One could read all about it in the Wall Street Journal and London's Financial Times. The drug importers did. No matter. The President of the United States, then the strongest, most powerful country in the world, pointed his finger at the map and, after some slight hesitation—

geography was never his strong point—called for immediate action against . . . Afghanistan.

Instantly, for the President of the United States commands tremendous assets, money and oil began to flow into the war machine. Money was oil and oil was money. A million gallons a day moved men and material across the Atlantic, carried them quickly through the Indian Ocean. And once again, the heroin began to flow from Afghanistan toward the United States of America.

An unexpected bonus of the U.S. invasion, though few in that nation's capital paid it much attention at the time, was that the supply of narcotic also reached the hospitals of Rwanda, Mali and other third-world countries where there were pressing needs.

Only a few weeks after Col. Gen. Khodaidad was brought in by the post-war Afghan government to be the new drug czar, though long enough afterward that the Bush administration could announce they were fighting drugs, they closed his offices and kicked the new czar's desk right out into the street. A month later, the Taliban, desperate for financing so that it could continue to repel the American invaders and retake its country, began to cultivate the very poppy fields it had destroyed a year before.

The United States persists in making all its old mistakes in Afghanistan.

The military's use of technology has been uneven. Drone aircraft rule the skies, though it's obvious from the number of civilian casualties that the United States is still in the learning stages as far as its application of drones is concerned. Though the United States has ruled the night via infrared technology since the Vietnam War, the attack on Camp Bastion by the Taliban in September 2012 was successful we are told because it was launched at night.

As in the second Gulf War, though the chief objective has been gained, the war continues. Thousands of Afghan civilians have been collateral damage. Hundreds of thousands have been turned by callous actions of military personnel into enemies. But what is perhaps most telling for America's future is that the military have appeared to relinquish control over their own troops.

The majority of Afghan civilians originally greeted the American invaders as saviors who would protect them from the excesses of the Taliban. But when they have seen friends and family members become collateral damage, the victims of drone strikes and misplaced attacks, when our troops lacking all sense of mission and direction burnt copies of the Koran, urinated on enemy corpses, and deliberately massacred civilians, few supporters are left.

More telling and with greater impact on our military's future: While the enlisted men who burnt copies of the Koran, urinated on enemy corpses, and deliberately massacred civilians have been singled out for punishment, not a single officer has been held accountable for his men's behavior.

The failure of command witnessed in Afghanistan has fatal implications for the likelihood of American success in potential combats against a larger and far more sophisticated enemy.

Money, Money, Money Makes the World Go Round

Money has always been the driving force in politics. Witness Mark Twain's 19th Century rants against a corrupt congress. The weapons makers have always been a driving force behind our wars, as Bernard Shaw described in his 1905 play Major Barbara.

Curiously, given the praise we heap on the members of our armed services (at least while there is a war on), the public is largely indifferent to the risk placed upon those same troops through the use of poorly-design weapons.

Union soldiers went to battle in shoddy uniforms that quickly fell apart. American soldiers fighting in Iraq went to battle in cardboard-thin "armored" vehicles.

And when it came to honoring our returning veterans, once again, we refer our readers to the quote from Kipling.

Because money is essential to reelection, money wins out over common sense. When missiles failed repeated tests during the second Iraq war, Bush Lite canceled the tests, and kept the U.S, buying the failed missiles.

When the Taliban halted poppy-growing in Afghanistan, the importers of illegal heroin, major backers of the Bush administration, complained bitterly. The United States invaded Afghanistan and soon heroin was back on the streets of New York and every other urban ghetto. The new producers were the Taliban who used the funds from the sale of crude heroin to fund their cause.

After 9/11/2001, Bush immediately told the American people he would confiscate the funds of those who had financed the terrorists' attacks. But the Saudi's have always been major contributors to the Bush campaigns. When Bush found out that both the attackers and those who had financed them were Saudis, he immediately forgot about his promise.

As the result of the intervention of money in politics, we no longer fight to win.

Our military engagements since the Second World War have amply demonstrated that the United States does not invade a country in order to defeat an enemy but only to justify both maintaining a bloated military and continuing to purchase large amounts of material of indifferent quality in its support.

Often, we are defeated before we start, attacking in the absence of any clear-cut plan or, indeed, of knowing just how to identify the enemy.

It is easy enough to declare victory in Iraq aboard a ship off the coast of San Diego, when the nature of "victory" remains undefined. When "enemy" and "ally" both look the same and speak the same language as they do in Korea, Vietnam, South America, Iraq, and Afghanistan, our soldiers and their officers are confused and mental breakdowns common. When we humiliate the enemy by burning their holy books or spitting on their corpses), all our allies see in the resulting photographs are men and women like themselves.

How long can our country support the back-breaking expense of our military?

The Hidden Costs of War

We've already commented on the size of our military's payroll, to which need be added the cost of base and off-base housing—the latter includes a 15,000-square-foot, 19th century chateau in Belgium, a 6,600-square-foot villa in Naples, and 19th century plantation house in New Orleans listed on the National Register of Historic Places--the maintenance of grounds and golf courses in over 168 countries, cost of contractors when contactors are used to supplement our troops for base security, the cost of fuel, and the cost of any and all equipment (whether or not in working order) designated for military use only.

But the expense does not end when a veteran is discharged. Medical care, education, and retraining for civilian work is (or ought to be) provided.[3]

According to Paul Sullivan, formerly Executive Director at Veterans for Common Sense, as of May 2012, the United States Department of Defense (DoD) deployed approximately 2.4 million individual active duty service members to the war zones in and around Iraq since September 2001. Of those, more than 1.6 million were discharged from active duty and are now veterans. As veterans, they are eligible for healthcare and disability benefits provided by the U.S. Department of Veterans Affairs (VA). Specifically, our recently deployed veterans receive five years of free VA medical care starting from the date of the veteran's discharge from active duty, a

---

[3] In September, 2012 the U.S. Senate shelved a veterans employment bill under pressure from Republicans.

new benefit that began in 2009. For comparison, the U.S. deployed 700,000 to the 1990 - 1991 Gulf War, 3.4 million to the Vietnam War, and 1.8 million to the Korean War, and there were few re-deployments for those three prior wars.

But the largest hidden cost is the restriction of Americans' civil liberties.

Today, proof of citizenship or legal entry is required to leave the U.S. and a passport is required to reenter the country (so much for a quick daytrip to the United States' Canadian and Mexican neighbors).

The USA Patriot Act of 200, reauthorized by Congress in 2011, provides for all of the following:

- Roving wiretaps
- Searches of "any tangible thing" (including bank and credit card records, internet history, and library borrowings)
- "Sneak-and-peek" warrants that permit law enforcement to raid a suspect's house without notifying the recipient of the intrusion
- Surveillance of individuals not related to terrorist groups.

Here is but a single example of the Act's misapplication, as cited by Walter Brasch: The FBI interviewed all Muslims in Moscow, Idaho and then arrested a graduate student in computer science. They claimed he aided terrorists by acting as webmaster for an Islamic charity. They held him in prison for sixteen months before trial and threatened him with a potential 25-year sentence. A jury found him not guilty after a two-month trial.

Fearing a similar result for the suspects held at Guantanamo in Cuba, the military has refused to turn them over to civilian courts.

A Legacy of Failure

What have we gained from the past twenty years of expenditures? In Afghanistan, more than 38,000 women and children were killed in 2013. In Iraq, suicide bombers killed 1000 people in July 2013 alone. The populations of both countries agree on only one thing, their hatred of Americans based on their contact with our out-of-control troops who rape and murder at will.

Curiously, only enlisted men and non-commissioned officers have been arrested, the over-paid commanding officers on their chains of command have never once been held responsible:

Marine Sgt. Larry Hutchins received an 11-year sentence for killing an unarmed Iraqi. His commanding officer wasn't charged.

Four soldiers from a Stryker brigade out of Lewis-McChord, Washington, were sent to prison in connection with the 2010 killings of three unarmed men during patrols in Kandahar province's Maiwand district. They were accused of forming a "kill team" that murdered Afghan civilians for sport. Their commanding officers at Lewis-McChord were held blameless.

Robert Bales killed 16 Afghan civilians including three women and nine children. His commanding officers were permitted to remain nameless and blameless.

Private Bradley Manning, who looks barely-old enough to shave, will spend most of his young life in a military prison, convicted on multiple charges for giving classified material to Wikileaks. His commanding officers, who left Manning free to do whatever he wanted, and thereby endangered America's entire diplomatic credibility--were not charged.

The United States military has lost all credibility abroad and at home. The world's failure to halt the Syrian genocide demonstrated that the lies Bush told resulted in every European country automatically distrusting America's pronouncements. As for the American people, themselves, today, four out of five Americans:

- Oppose military action abroad
- Want to maintain the size of America's top-heavy military
- Want their government to continue to purchase weapons even if it means doing without essential social services
- Are unwilling to pay for veterans' medical expenses.

The Elephant in the Room

While the United States has sacrificed its infra-structure--its roads, its sewer pipes, its social services, to pay for a bloated military, China has undergone a slow period of expansion in all areas. China now had 2.29 million persons in its military, while the United States has 1.48 million at a cost of 1.65% and 4.7% of their gross domestic products respectively.

During the past thirty years for every factory that closed in the United States displacing hundreds sometimes thousands of once-employed workers, China has opened two factories. Today, what remains of manufacturing plants in the United States are rapidly been acquired by China.

In countries where the United States has established military bases, China is conducting its own courtships by building roads, harbors, and other development projects. In the long term, China will surely replace the U.S. as the dominant world power. Unless war between the two countries takes place first.

In September 2012, "spontaneous" demonstrations in several major Chinese cities were directed against both the Japanese government and Japanese businesses. The pretext for these demonstrations was the Japanese government's insistence that certain islands in the South China Sea, owned and occupied by Japanese citizens for more than a hundred years, were part of Chinese territory. These tiny rocky islets are virtually uninhabitable; their attraction lies in their location in an area of the ocean that is home to an abundance of fish and thought to be rich in minerals.

Protests in countries controlled by communists are never "spontaneous," they are always organized by the government and their ranks filled by "volunteers" from the civil service. The recent protests were to be expected as China claims the islands as their own territory, citing maps go back hundreds of years. (The prospect of the Chinese' Government's claim being accepted by the international community is a scary one, as evidence unearthed by Gavin Menzies suggests that the Chinese were the first to explore the West Coast of the Americas, landing on our shores as early as 1421.)

Were these protests directed at Japan or at its close ally, the United States? In that same month, China accused the U.S. of attempting to encircle its country militarily.

This accusation was not unjustified. The Obama Administration is forging closer ties with India, Vietnam, Indonesia and Singapore, repositioning troops, planes and ships. They are negotiating to regain access to Subic Bay and Clark Air Force Base in the Philippines. Marines and jet fighters are on their way to Guam, Hawaii, Okinawa, and northern Australia. Of course, the U.S. still has several divisions located close to the border between Northern and Southern Korea.

Unfortunately, the net effect of all these additional troops may be to drive the U.S. further into bankruptcy.

What Can Be Done?

The Soviet Union collapsed for two reasons:
1. Their economy could not support the arms race their cold war with America entailed, and their costly and failed incursion into Afghanistan was the coup de gras.
2. The first generation of Soviet politicians who survived the death of Stalin consisted in the main of hardworking Stankovites; their children were dissolute coke-snorting wastrels. If they wanted their country to survive, and they did, they had no choice but to let the various soviets go their separate ways.

One can see some interesting parallels with our own plight.
1. Our arms race, seemingly with every other country in the world as a competitor, has brought us to the brink of bankruptcy, and our costly and failed incursion into Afghanistan may have sealed our fate.
2. The abolishment of the estate tax in the United States has led to an unprecedented consolidation of wealth in America and to the development of a privileged second generation whose only though is not what they could do for their country but what their country can do for them. Contrast the thoughtful first President Bush, capable of striking a careful

balance between strategy and tactics, with his wastrel Congressman's son who never completed a job in his life.[4]

The two obvious solutions to America's current dilemma are to cut back on military spending and to reinstate the estate tax. But ask any junkie, knowing what to do and doing it are two quite different things.

To trim military spending on weapons, <u>Dina Rasor</u> says three changes are essential:

- Get control of the money flow. The Pentagon has not passed an overall fiscal audit in decades, nor is one due until 2017!
- Change the way weapons are priced to what they *should* cost, not what they have cost in the past.
- Advance a weapon into full production only after all tests are completed successfully.

What kind of money are we talking about? Since the onset of "the Global War on Terror" in 2001, the total cost for our garrisoning policies, for our presence abroad (and the U.S had more than 1,000 bases abroad with about 4,000 more in the 50 states and Washington, D.C) has probably reached $1.8 trillion to $2.1 trillion.

True, the annual "Overseas Cost Summary" or the 2012 fiscal year ending September 30th, documented $22.1 billion in spending, although, at Congress's direction, this doesn't include any of the more than $118 billion spent that year on the wars in Afghanistan and

---

[4] See Chapter 7 of Craig Unger's <u>House of Bush, House of Saud</u>.

elsewhere around the globe. Nor does the Summary include any of the following expenditures:

- $3.6 billion for territories and Pacific island nations.
- $5.3 billion for Navy vessels and personnel plus seaborne and airborne assets.
- $12.6 billion for health care, military and family housing, shopping and postal subsidies.
- $6.9 billion in net "rent" payments and NATO contributions.
- $13.6 billion for classified programs, military intelligence, and CIA paramilitary activities.
- $104.9 billion for bases and military presence in Afghanistan and other war zones.

Isn't it about time the U.S. brought its troops home?

Next, you, the voter, need to ask Congress and the President to reduce the size of the military, *trimming from the top down.* By the end of March 2010, the Armed Services held 950 officers of flag rank, 38 four-stars, 149 three-stars, 299 two-stars and 464 one-stars, plus a myriad of officers to order a still larger group of noncoms and enlisted men and women to do their bidding.

Four-star officers earn a maximum of 180 thousand dollars a year, and retire after 40 years in uniform with a $237 thousand a dollars a year pension. They often reward themselves with lavish perks including personal aides, cooks, drivers and around-the-world trips with family and friends.[5]

What do these 38 four stars do? More to the point what do they accomplish? Is the U.S. really at war or preparing for war in 48 battle fields? In WWII, there was one officer to every ten enlisted men. Today, there are two officers for every enlisted man.

But in WWII, incompetent commanders were fired and replaced by quality men at division and regiment. By the latter part of the Korean War and in America's wars in Vietnam, Afghanistan, and Iraq, relief of generals by generals became seldom occurred. In Afghanistan, enlisted men urinate on corpses, burn books holy to the indigenous population, and murder innocent women and children, but not a single officer is held responsible for the troops under his command.

I repeat, write your Congressperson and tell him or her to ignore the campaign contributions he or she receives from weapons manufacturers and urge the President to trim our bloated military from the top down.

Not a chance your Congressperson will follow through? You're probably right. Anyone familiar with the writings of Mark Twain is well aware of the contempt with which he held Congress two centuries ago. But there is a major difference between the Congresspersons of his day and ours: In his day, they were for sale only to the highest American bidder. Today, Congress is open to be

---

[5] Theoretically, they function under civilian control, but no defense secretary has actually reined in the generals' lavish spending.

bought by the Arabs, the Chinese, and multi-national corporations whose interests may or may coincide with ours. The <u>Citizens United decision</u> has only enabled further foreign interference in U.S. affairs.

At one time in America, politics and the surrounding corruption were local. Gifts to your local officials could assure government contracts. A vote as well as precinct work on behalf of your local politicians could assure a later government appointment. But with the advent of radio and later of television, the support of individual voters was no longer obtained through jobs, but via advertising puffery over national media. Only money and the monies' donors remained to dominate campaigns.

Still later in the 20th Century, financial considerations from multi-national corporations and from other nations exceeded anything that all but a small handful of American could contribute to campaign coffers. Curiously the American media while anxious to tell us about the campaign contributions of the Koch Brothers and Sherman Adelson has remained steadfastly silent about these contributions from abroad.

We have only one solution: Write your Congressional candidates today and let them know you will vote for them ONLY if they introduce and support Constitutional amendments to provide for both of the following:

- The death penalty for any Congressperson or military officer found to have accepted financial consideration from foreign interests.

- Restricting financial support for candidates for office to U.S. human citizens.

The United States has other problems. Americans differ on many issues and always will. Fortunately, the vast majority of Americans share a common desire for the future health of their country. But not all. Quislings can't wait to sell us out, for money, for their cause, or over one imagined grievance or the other.

When an individual banks most of his or her money in the Switzerland or the Caymans or invested in a multinational corporation, where else can his or her loyalties lie?

Once a Congressperson has lobbied to send more foreign aid to Saudi Arabia or to Pakistan, how difficult is to persuade this same person to pressure for the sharing of military secrets, or the admission of suspect individuals to our shores.

Although the terrorists who downed the Twin Towers and attempted to destroy the Pentagon were all Saudi Arabians, today visas for Saudis to visit the United States are issued by the Saudi Arabian government.

America has freedom of the press. But should this freedom be extended to foreign media? Yes and no. I say, yes, if like Al-Jazeera, they openly say they are owned by Qatar. I say, no, if like Fox News they conceal their ownership by China's PLA2.

It's up to you to take the next step.

In order to rule a people
You must first convince them they are only fit to
be ruled
On the first day, the people will laugh
On the second, they will protest
On the third, they will be convinced

Zanybooks.com invites you to comment on this book,
either on zanybooks' Facebook page or on the webpage
of the site where you purchased this text.